Happy Birthday

Harvey

Love

Nan & Granta

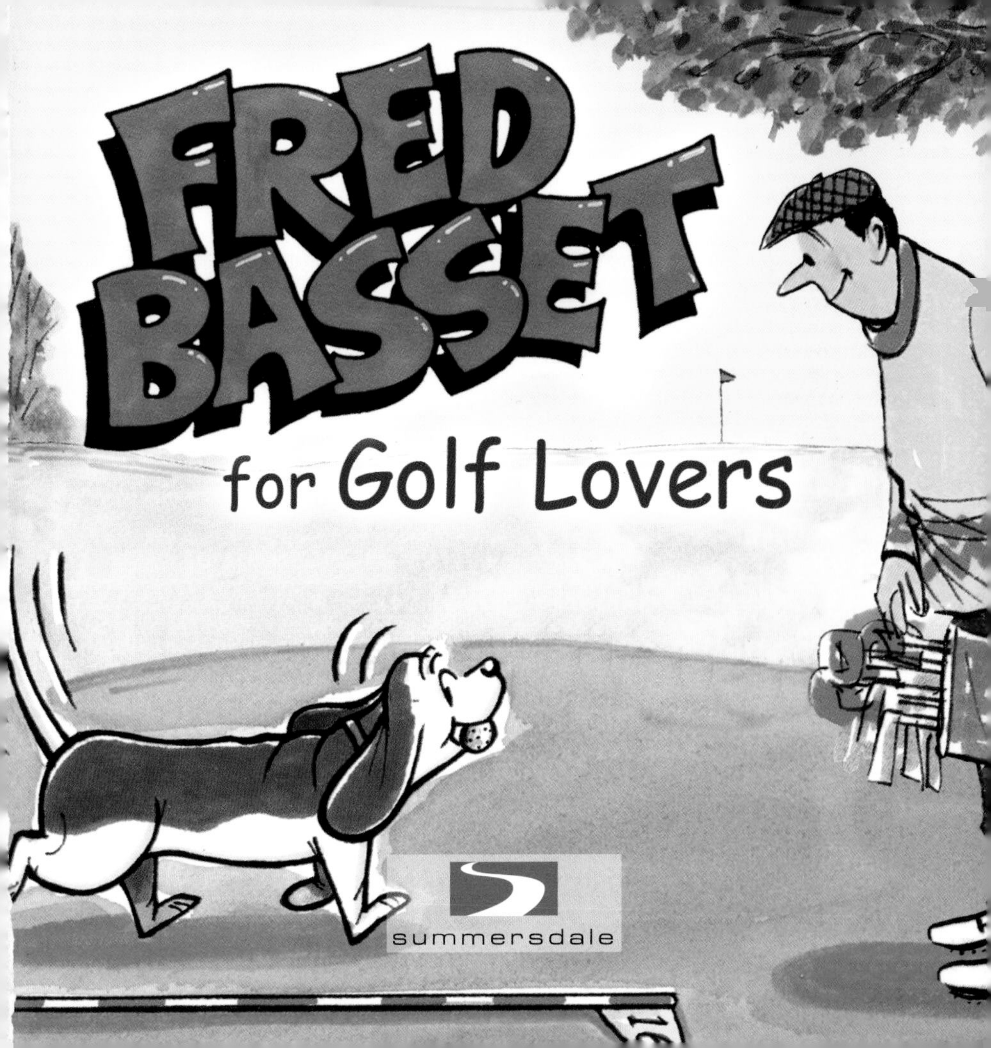
FRED BASSET
for Golf Lovers
summersdale

FRED BASSET

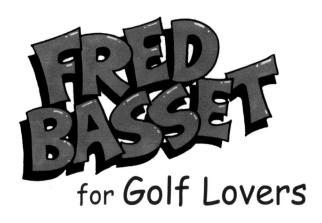

for Golf Lovers

Introducing Fred...

Fred Basset was created by Alex Graham in 1963, when he made his first appearance in the *Daily Mail*. He has held a regular spot in comic strips in the *Daily Mail* and *The Mail on Sunday* ever since. The popular pooch also features every year in calendars and has his very own annual, *The Fred Basset Yearbook*.

Fred Basset for Golf Lovers brings together the very best of Fred's golfing moments over the years, in a collection of full colour images never before gathered together in book form.

Fred makes the perfect golfing companion – he's certainly got a knack for finding lost golf balls and is on hand for moral support come rain or shine. He has plenty of fun on the fairway too, whether he's chasing a rabbit at the ninth hole or putting an opponent off mid-swing with a well-timed bark.

Of course, things don't always go smoothly, and the witty hound makes many a dry observation whilst waiting it out at the bunker. One thing's for sure – the annual golf dinner just wouldn't be the same without him making a guest appearance. Perhaps it's time they revised that rule about no dogs being allowed into the clubhouse...

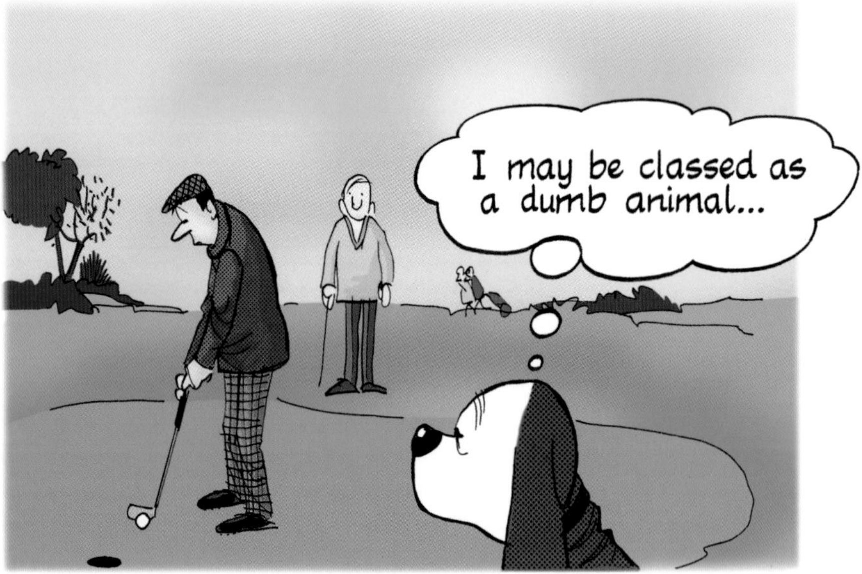
I may be classed as a dumb animal...

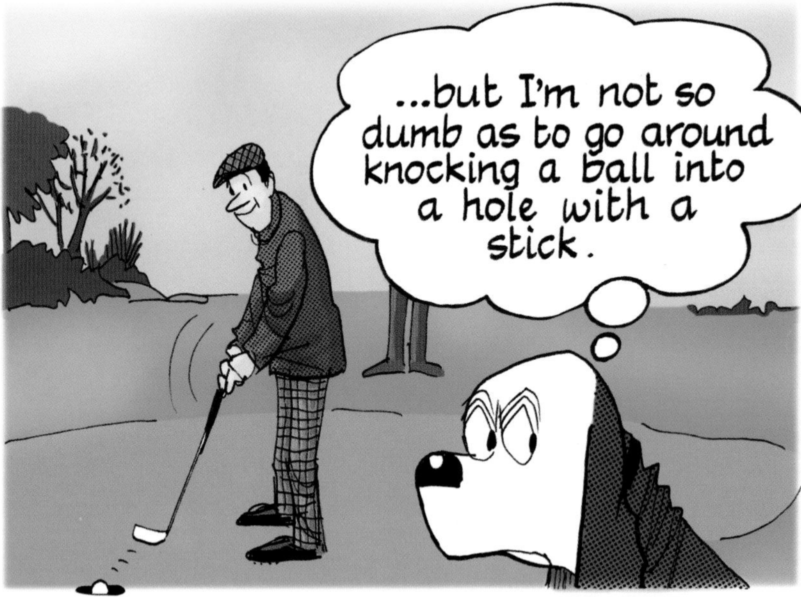
...but I'm not so dumb as to go around knocking a ball into a hole with a stick.

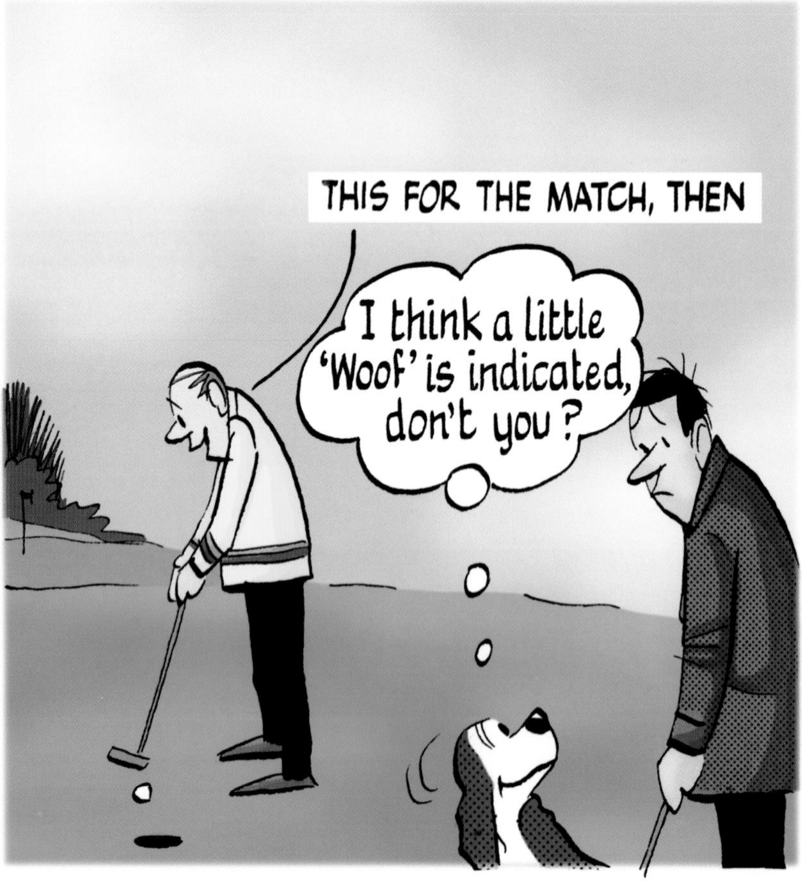
THIS FOR THE MATCH, THEN
I think a little 'Woof' is indicated, don't you?

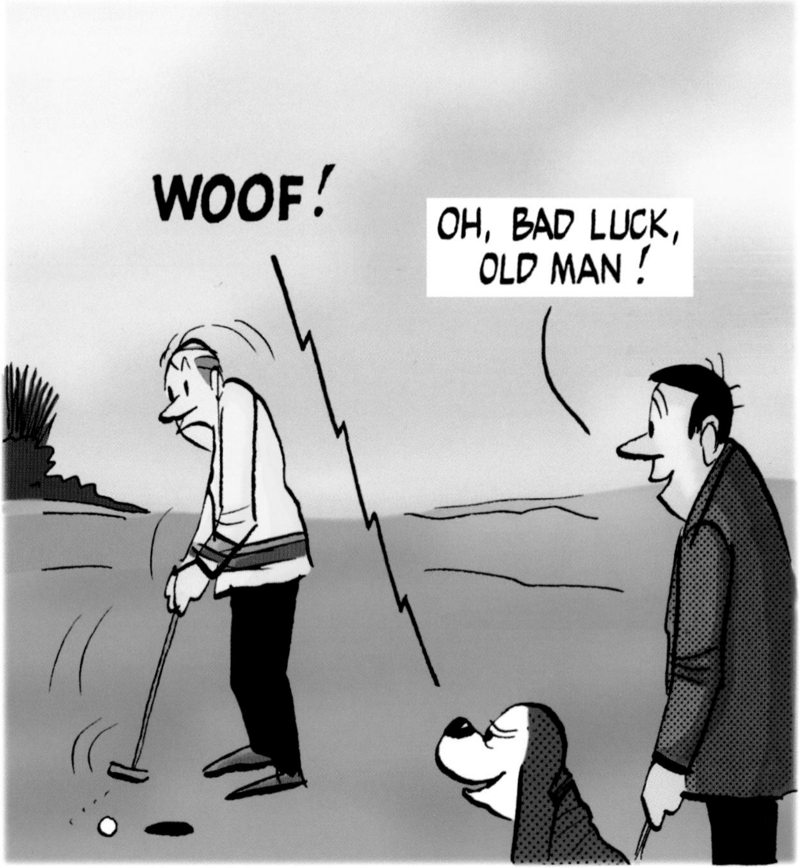
WOOF!
OH, BAD LUCK, OLD MAN!

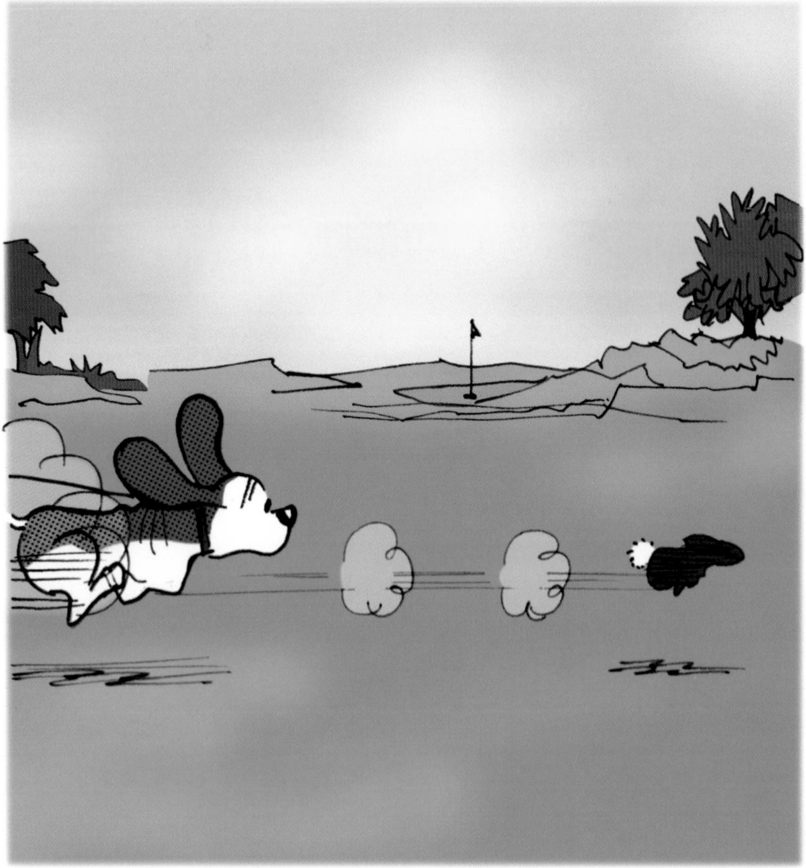

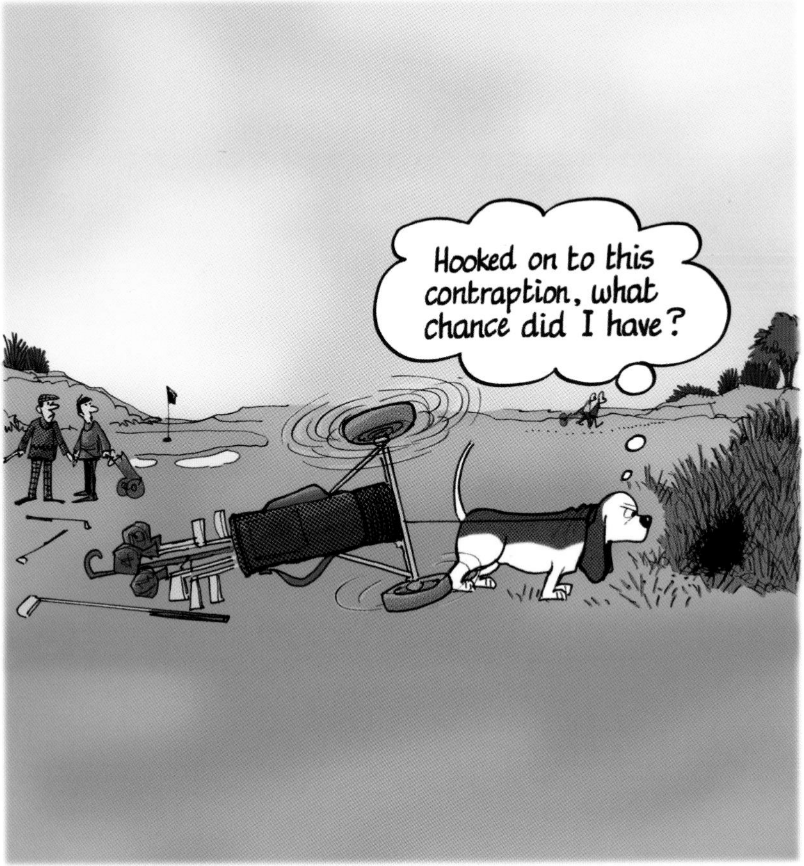
Hooked on to this contraption, what chance did I have?

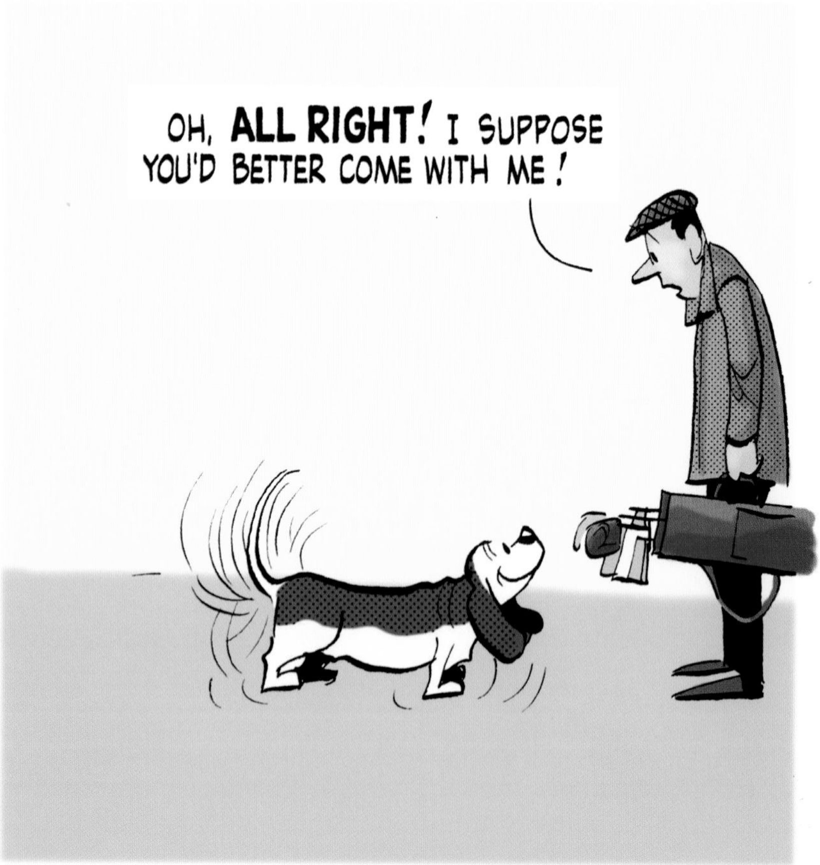
OH, ALL RIGHT! I SUPPOSE YOU'D BETTER COME WITH ME!

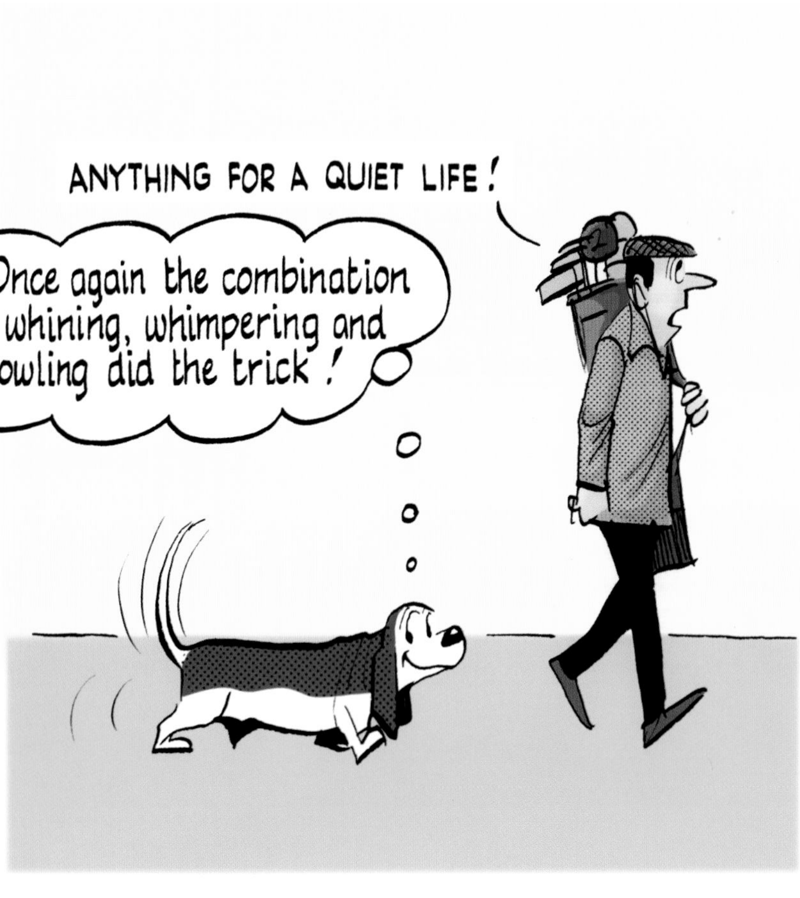
ANYTHING FOR A QUIET LIFE!
Once again the combination of whining, whimpering and howling did the trick!

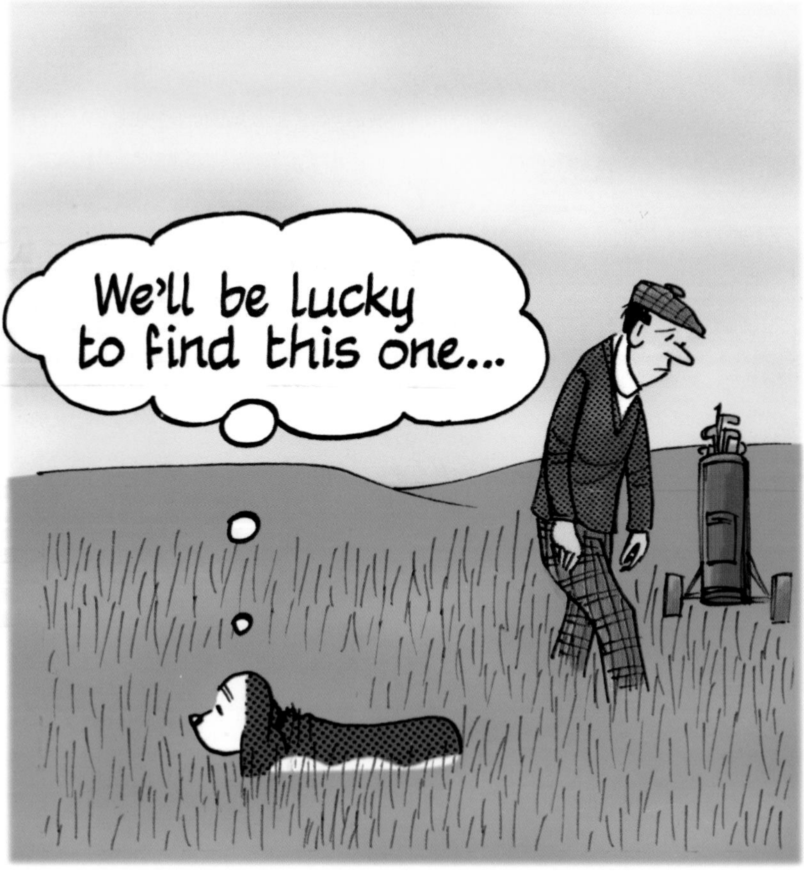
We'll be lucky to find this one...

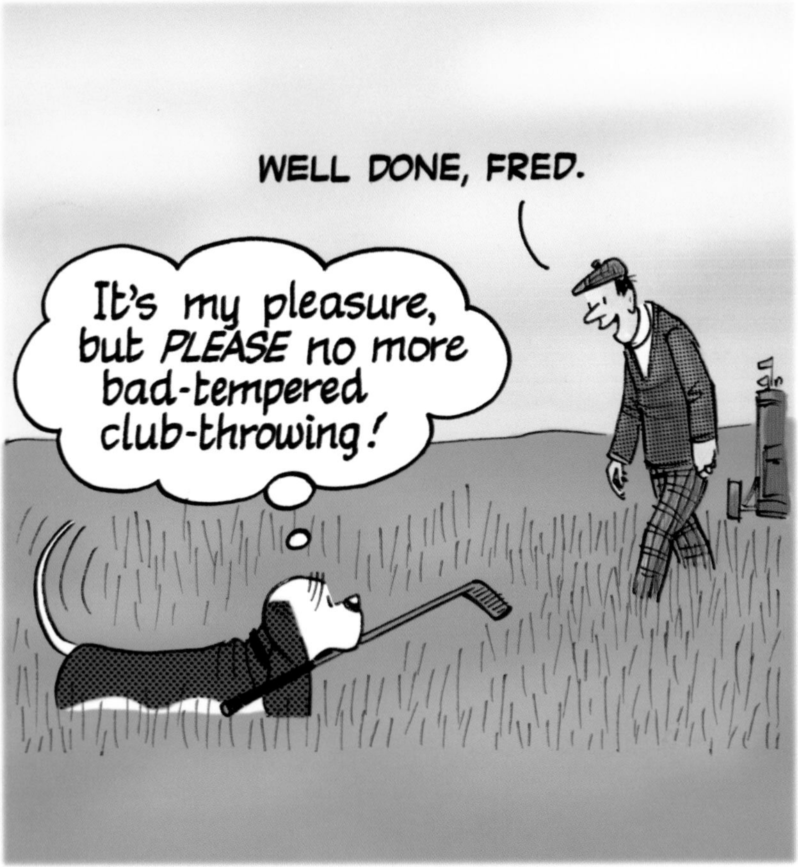
WELL DONE, FRED.
It's my pleasure, but PLEASE no more bad-tempered club-throwing!

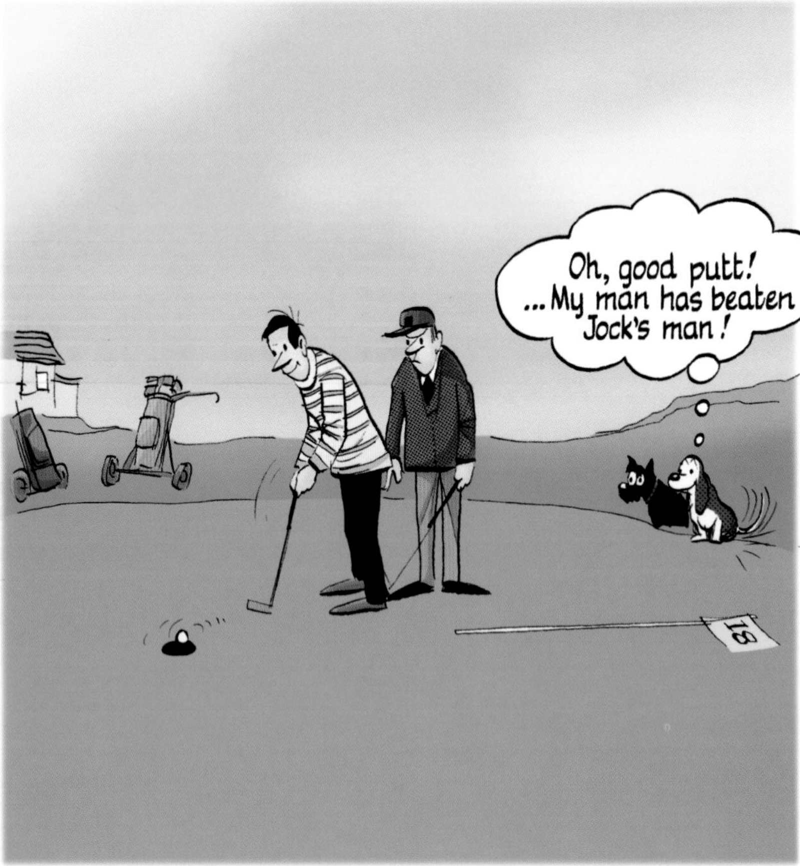
Oh, good putt! ...My man has beaten Jock's man!

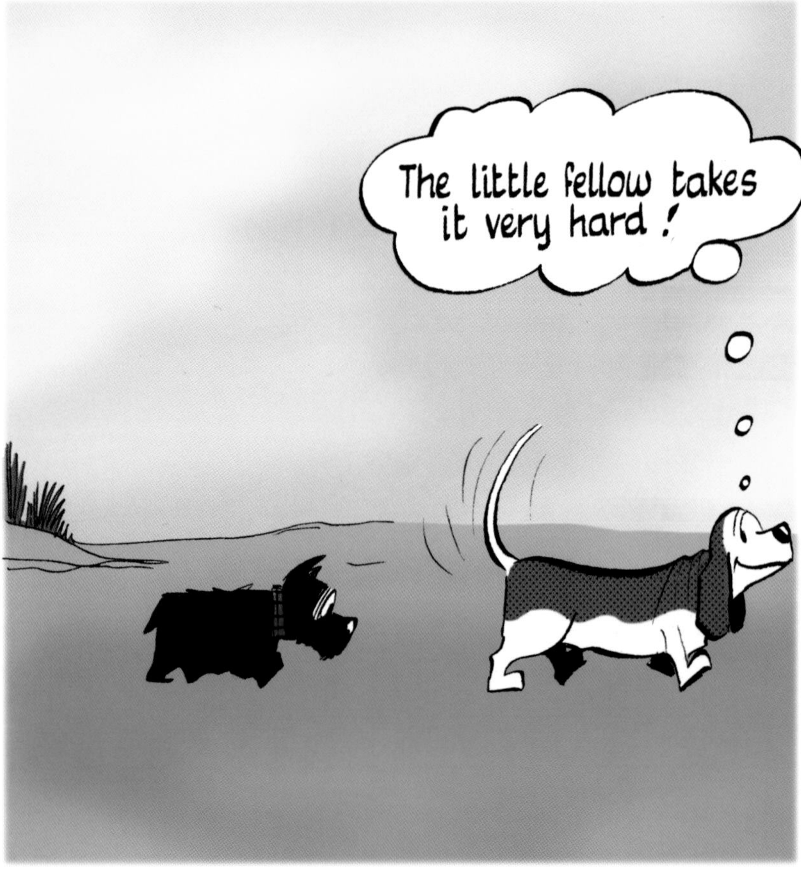
The little fellow takes it very hard!

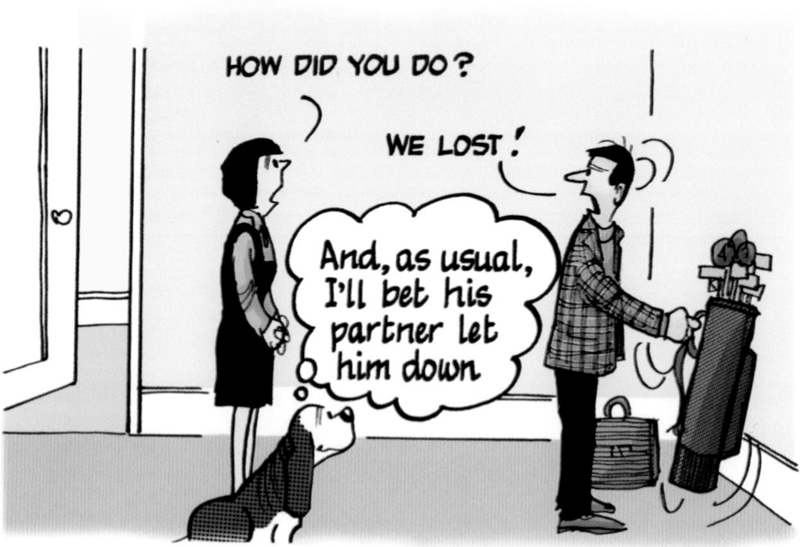
HOW DID YOU DO?
WE LOST!
And, as usual, I'll bet his partner let him down

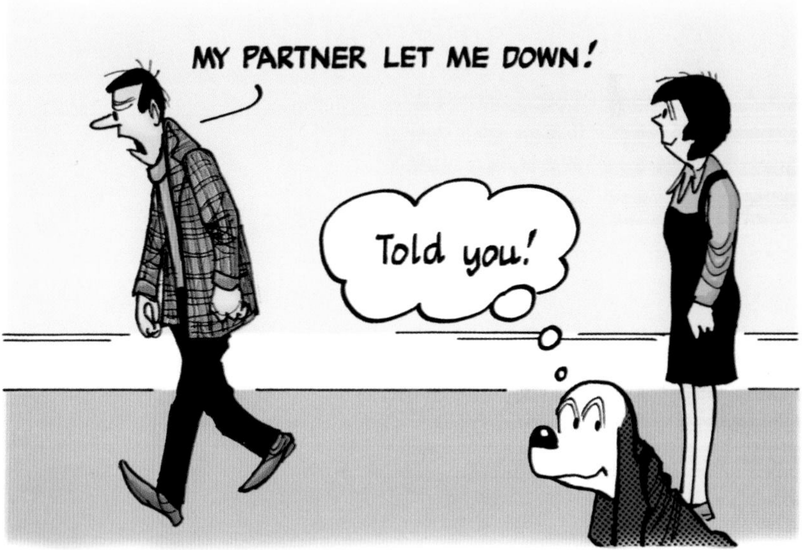
MY PARTNER LET ME DOWN!
Told you!

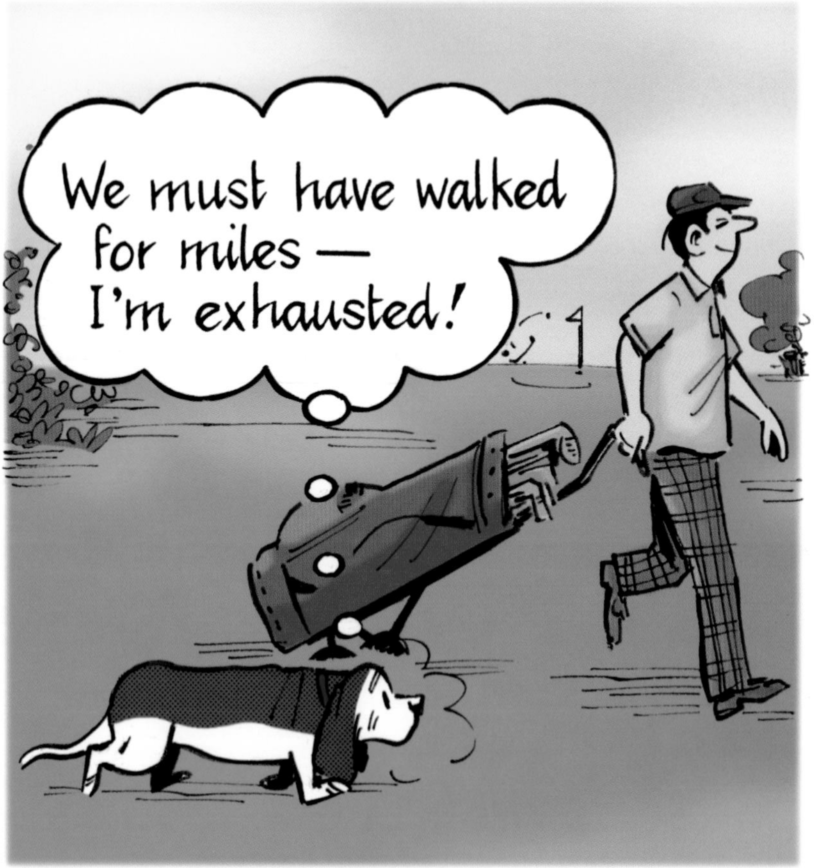
We must have walked for miles — I'm exhausted!

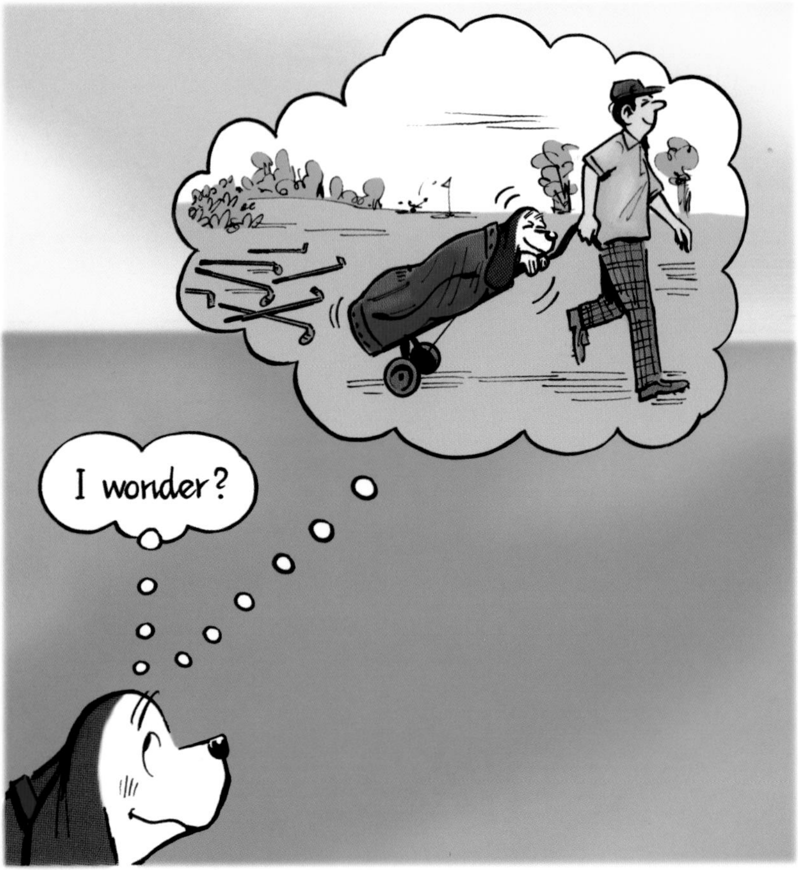
I wonder?

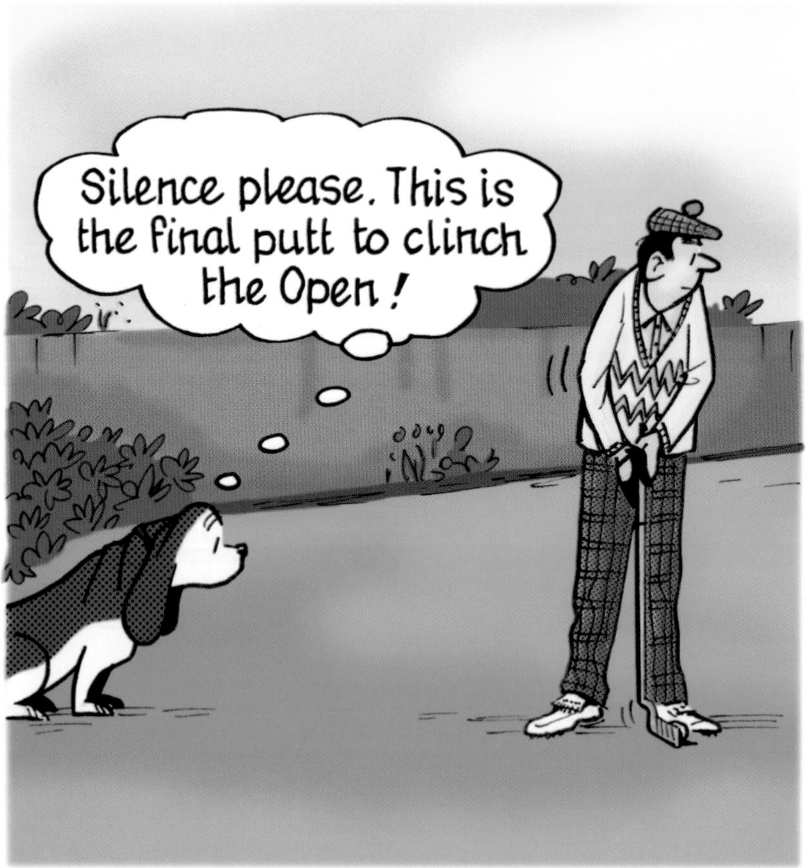
Silence please. This is the final putt to clinch the Open!

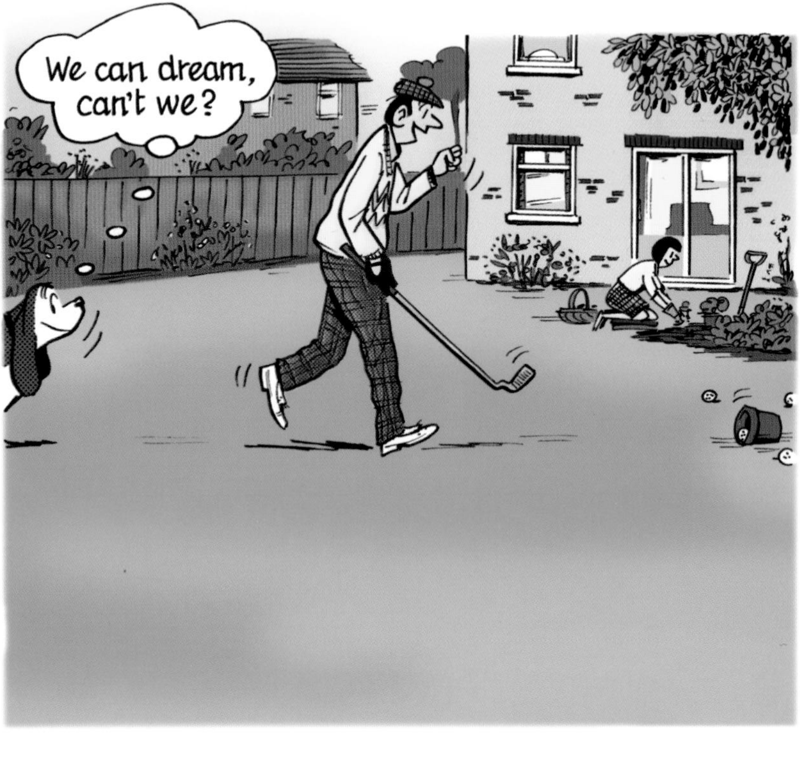
We can dream, can't we?

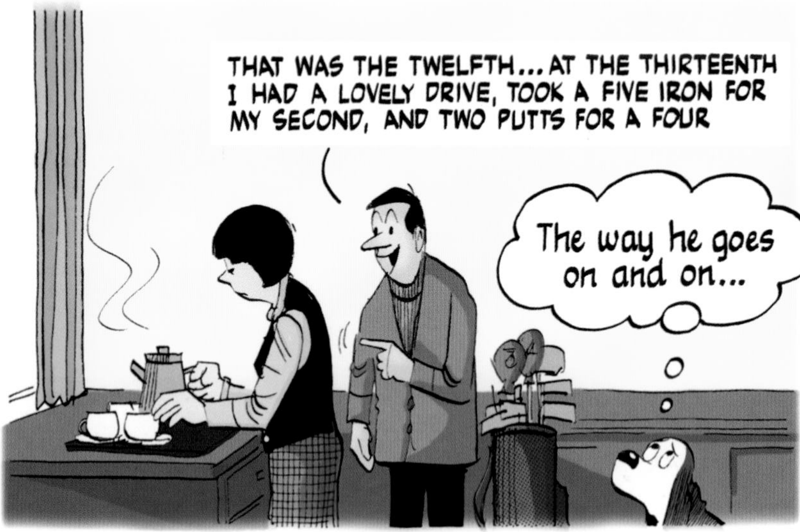

THAT WAS THE TWELFTH... AT THE THIRTEENTH I HAD A LOVELY DRIVE, TOOK A FIVE IRON FOR MY SECOND, AND TWO PUTTS FOR A FOUR
The way he goes on and on...

NOW WE COME TO THE SHORT FOURTEENTH...I HIT QUITE A GOOD TEE SHOT, ALMOST ON THE GREEN, AND...
If she was listening, I'll bet she'd be bored to tears

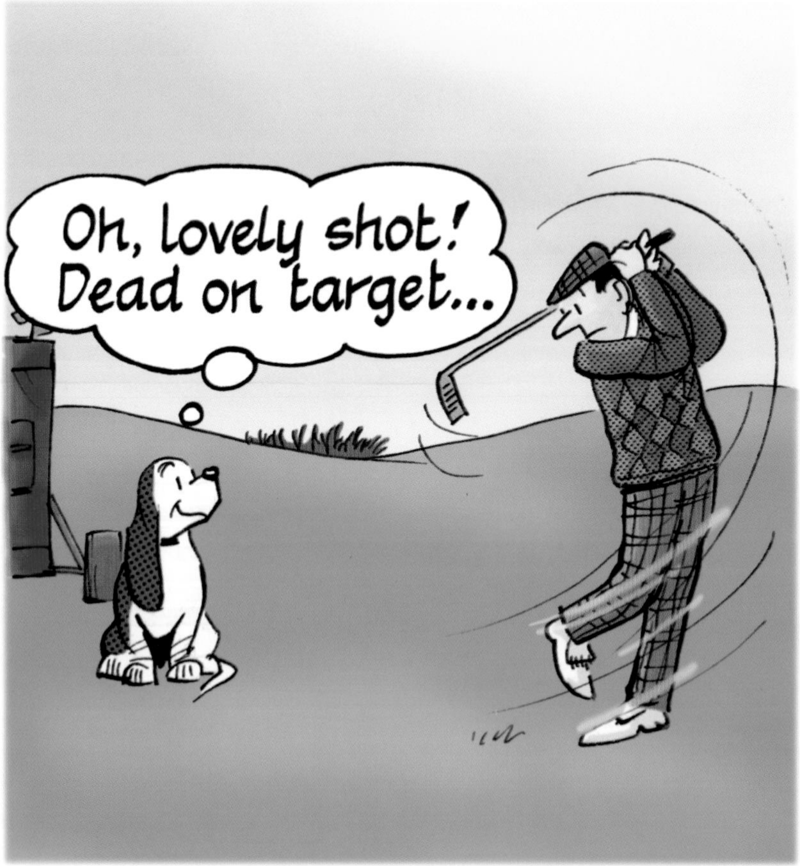
Oh, lovely shot! Dead on target...

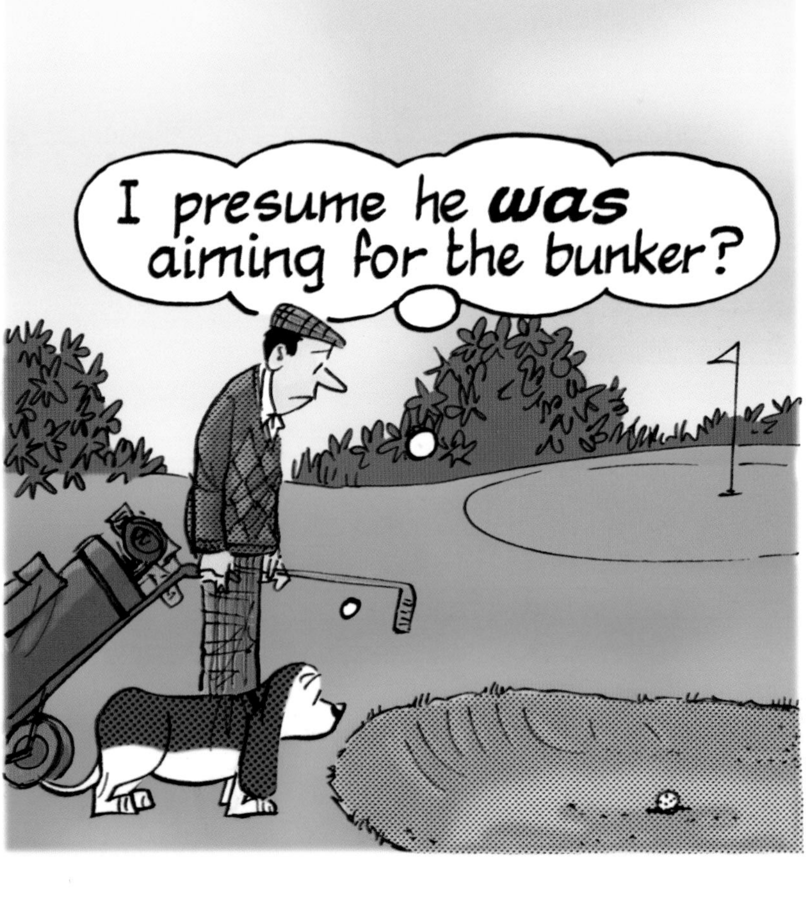
I presume he was aiming for the bunker?

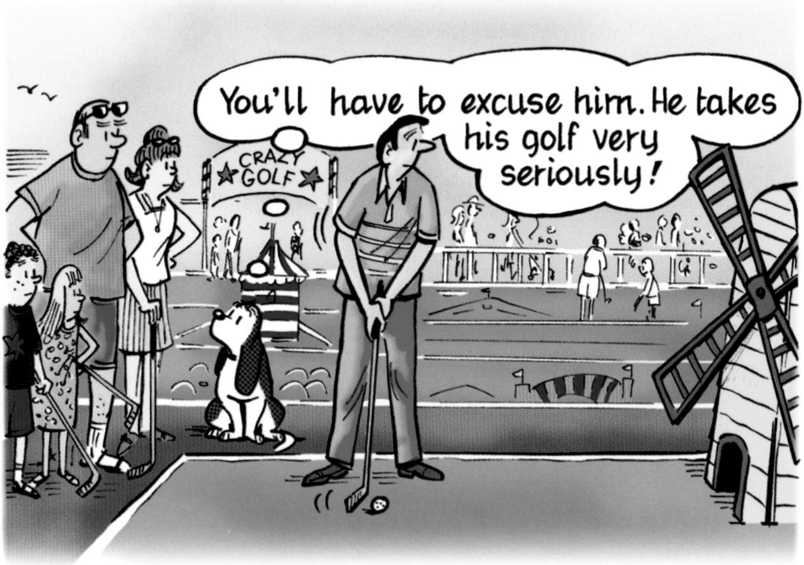
You'll have to excuse him. He takes his golf very seriously!
CRAZY GOLF

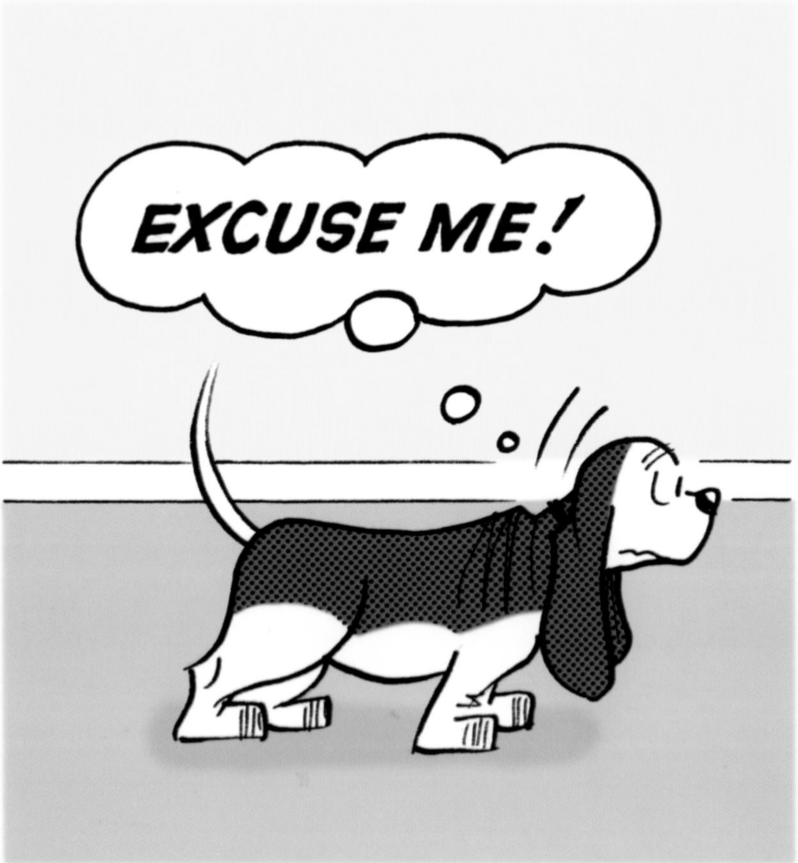
EXCUSE ME!

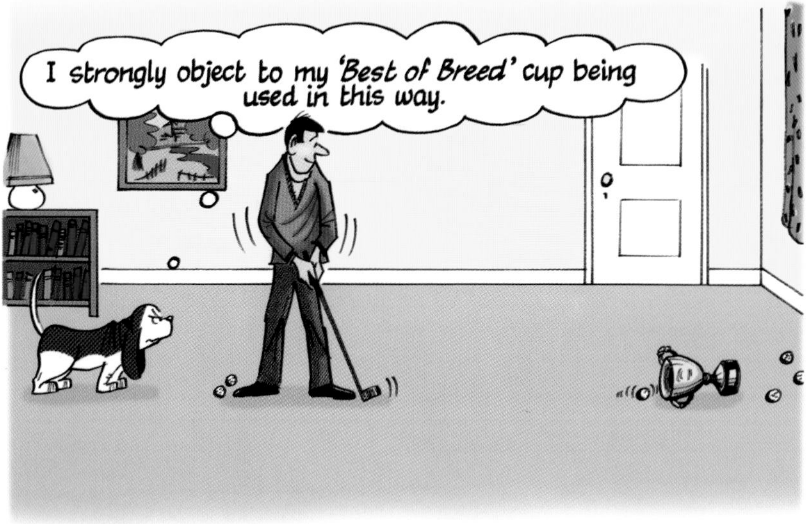
I strongly object to my 'Best of Breed' cup being used in this way.

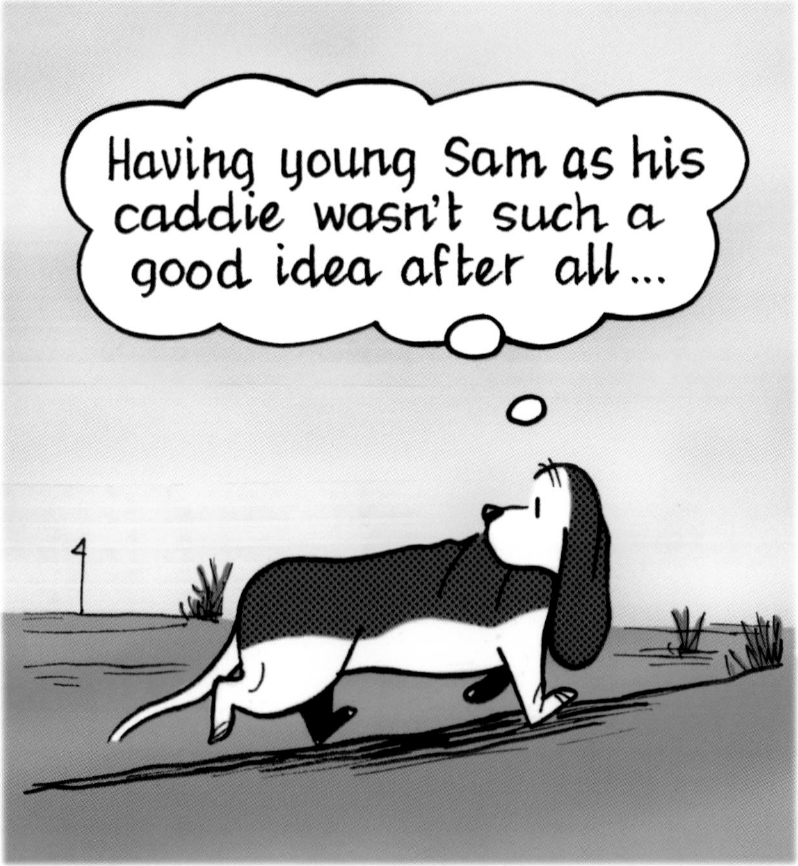
Having young Sam as his caddie wasn't such a good idea after all...
4

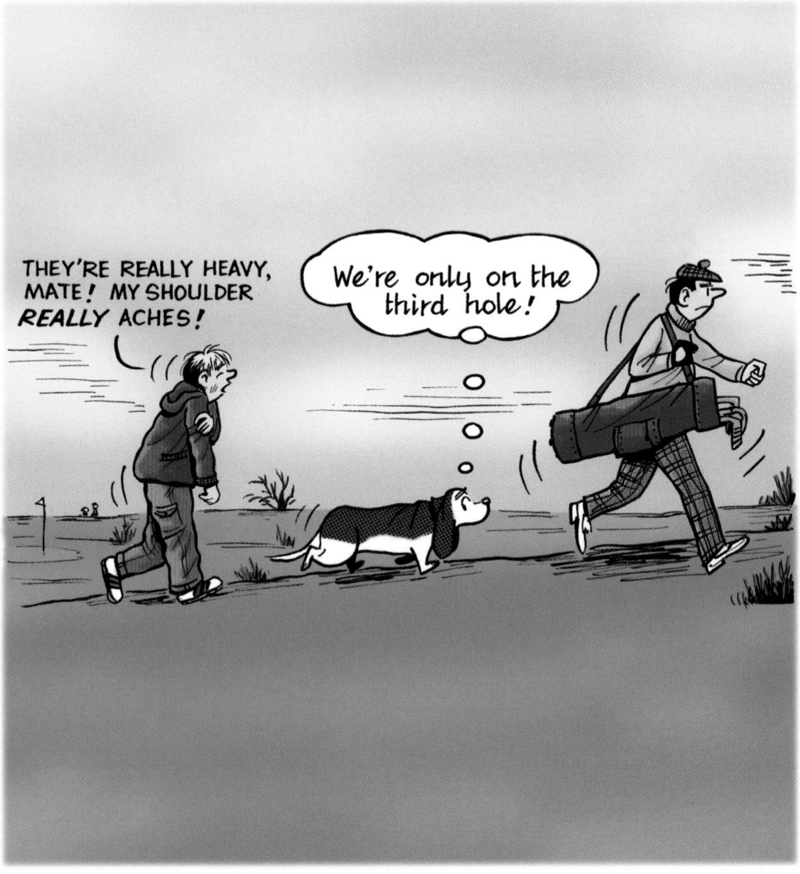
THEY'RE REALLY HEAVY, MATE! MY SHOULDER REALLY ACHES!
We're only on the third hole!

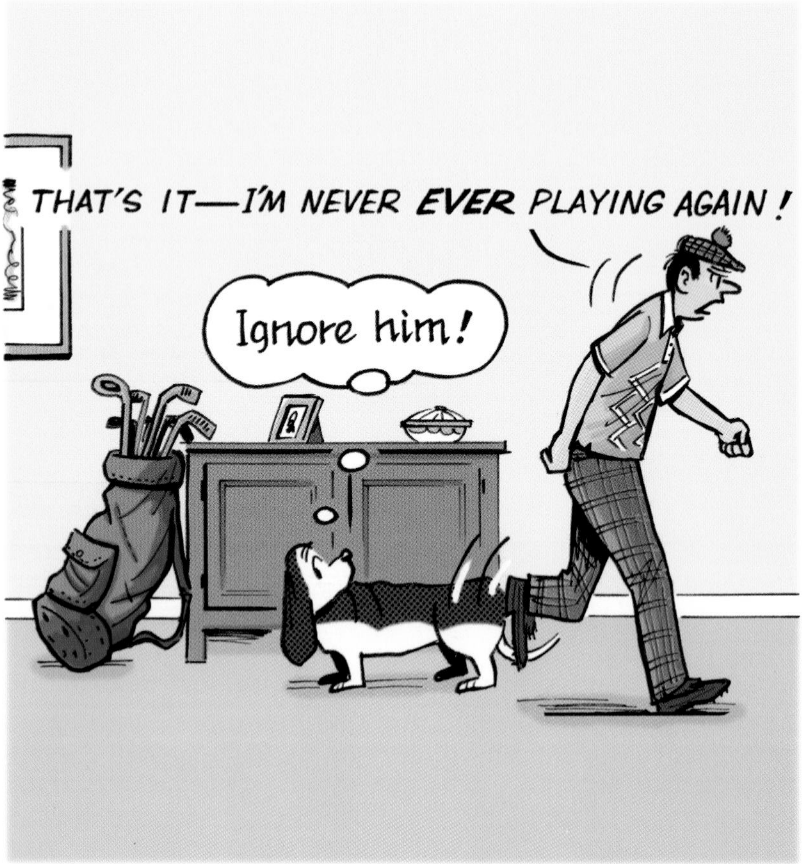
THAT'S IT—I'M NEVER EVER PLAYING AGAIN!
Ignore him!

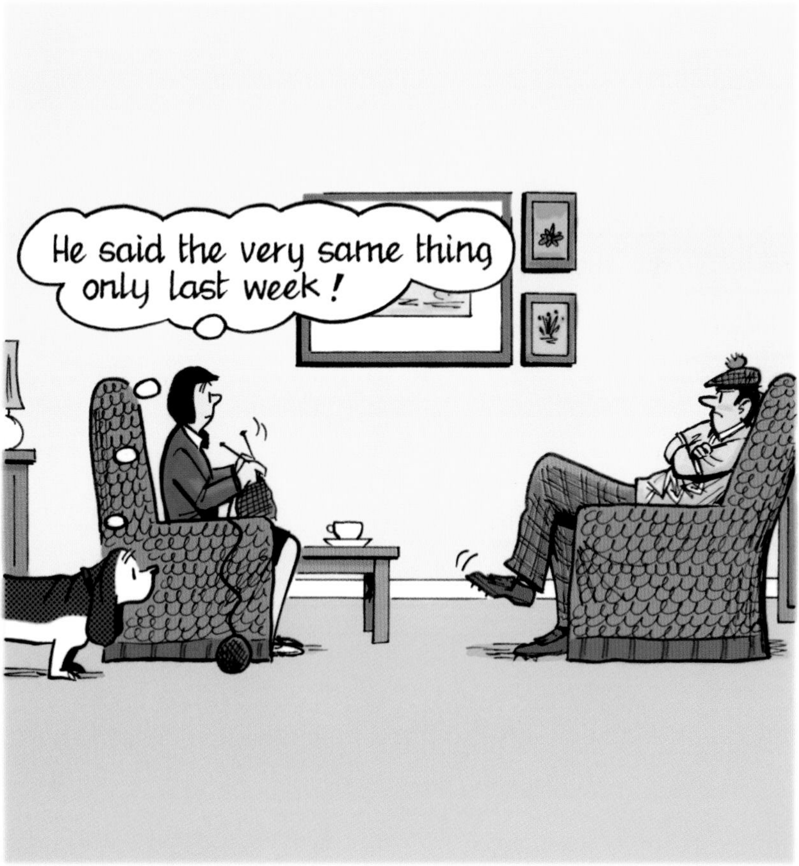
He said the very same thing only last week!

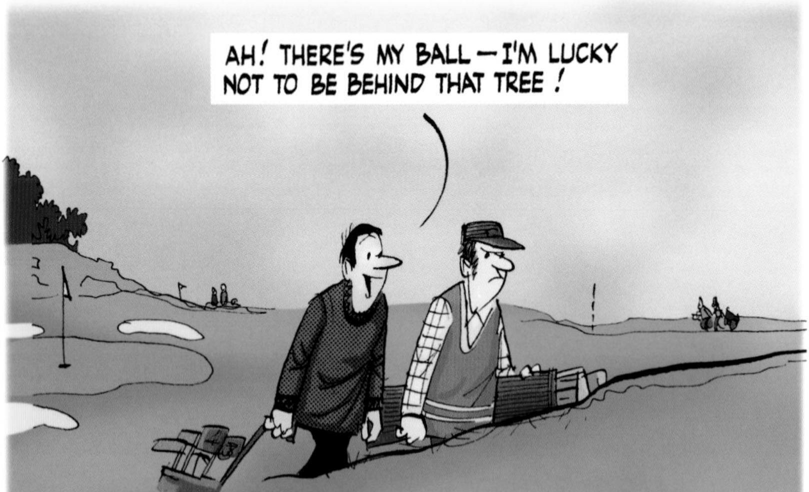
AH! THERE'S MY BALL — I'M LUCKY NOT TO BE BEHIND THAT TREE!

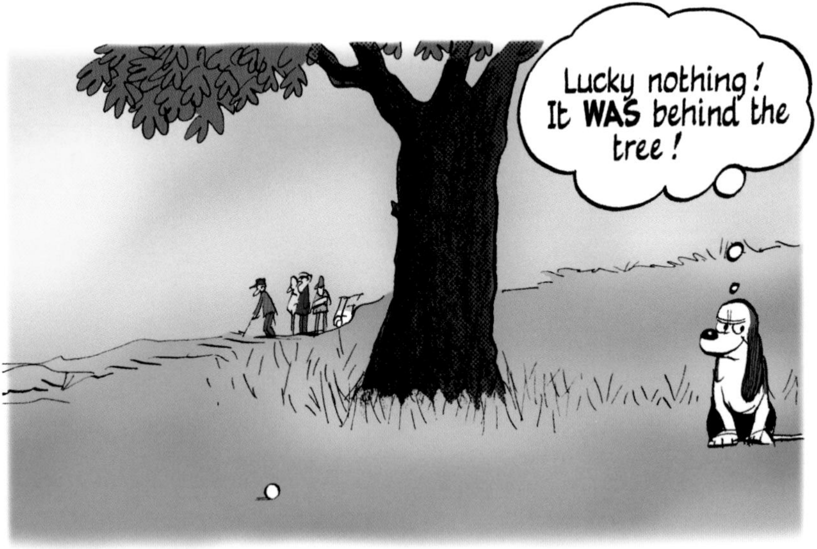
Lucky nothing! It WAS behind the tree!

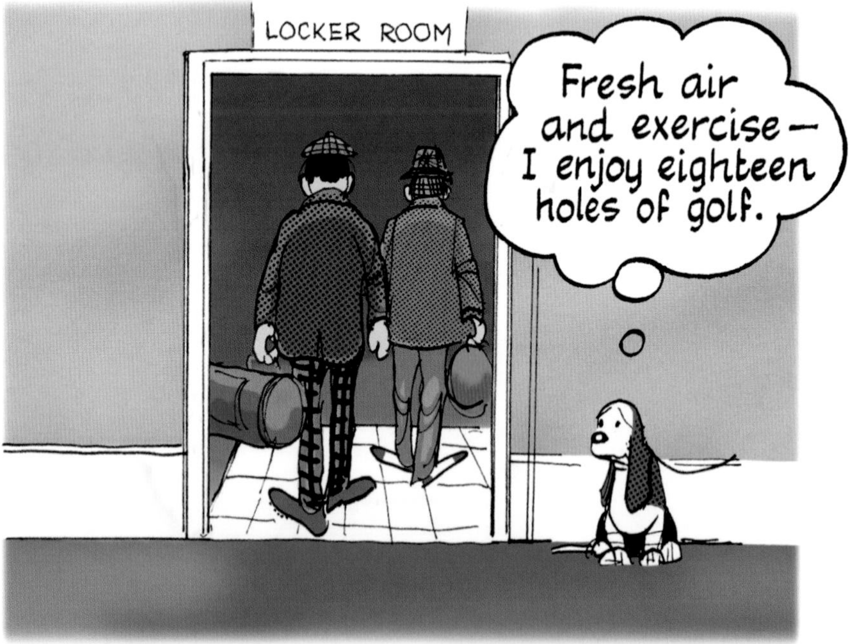
LOCKER ROOM
Fresh air and exercise— I enjoy eighteen holes of golf.

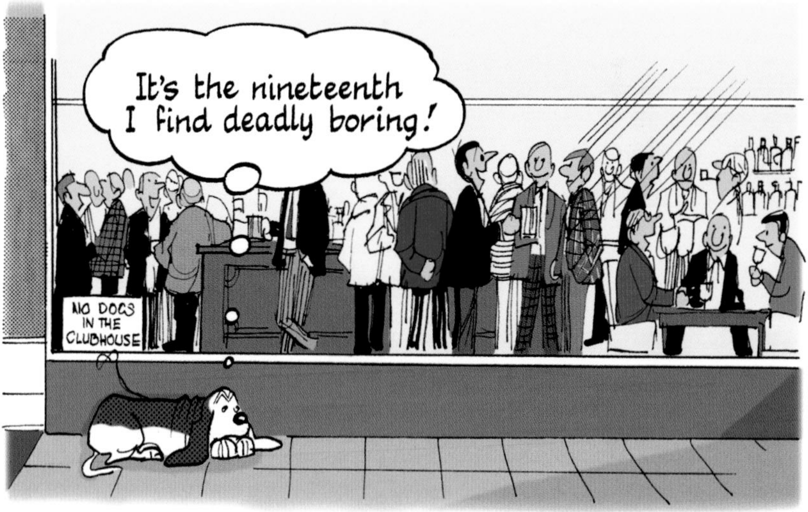
It's the nineteenth I find deadly boring!
NO DOGS IN THE CLUBHOUSE

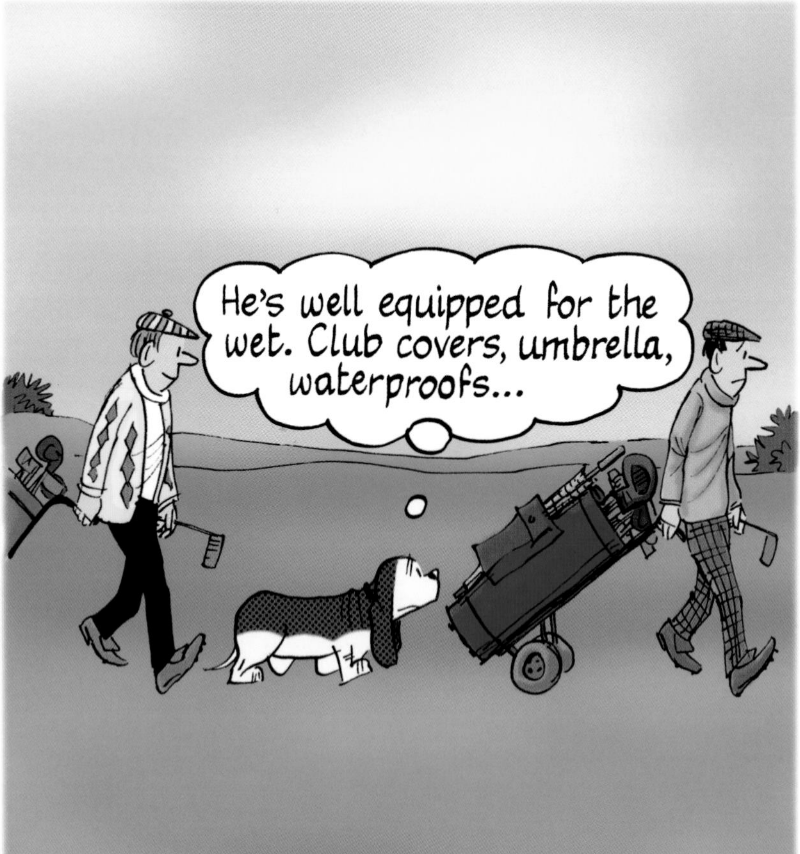
He's well equipped for the wet. Club covers, umbrella, waterproofs...

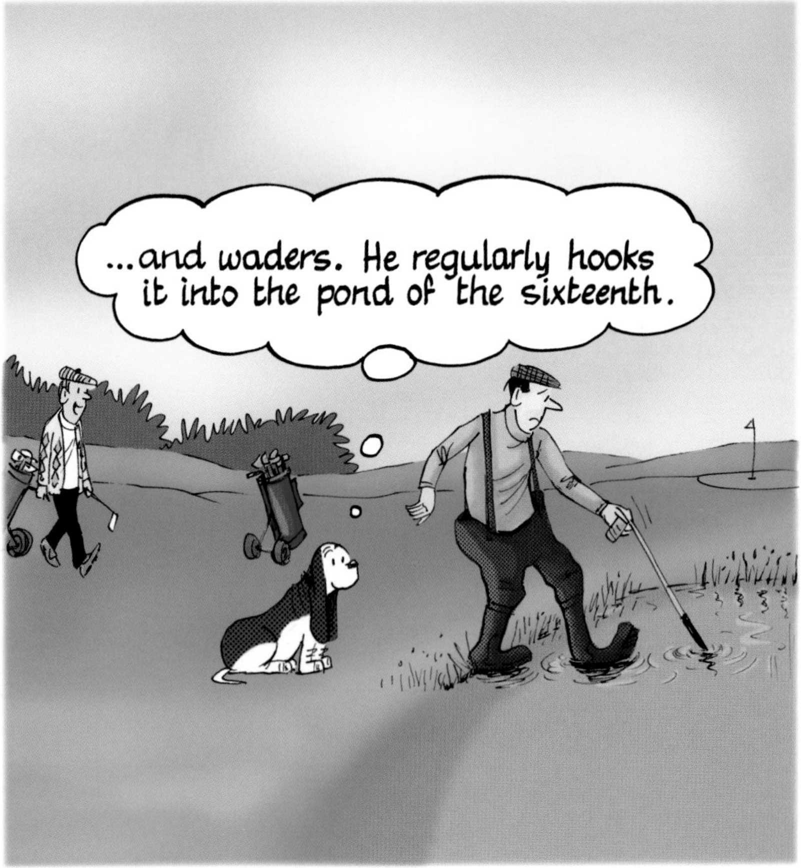
...and waders. He regularly hooks it into the pond of the sixteenth.

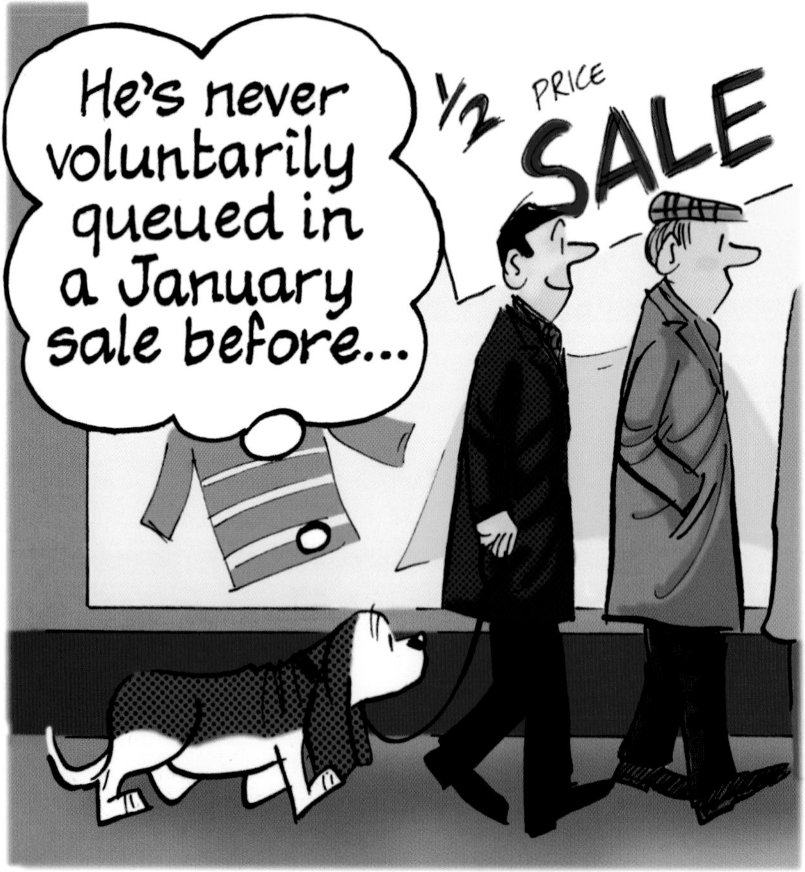
He's never voluntarily queued in a January sale before...
1/2 PRICE SALE

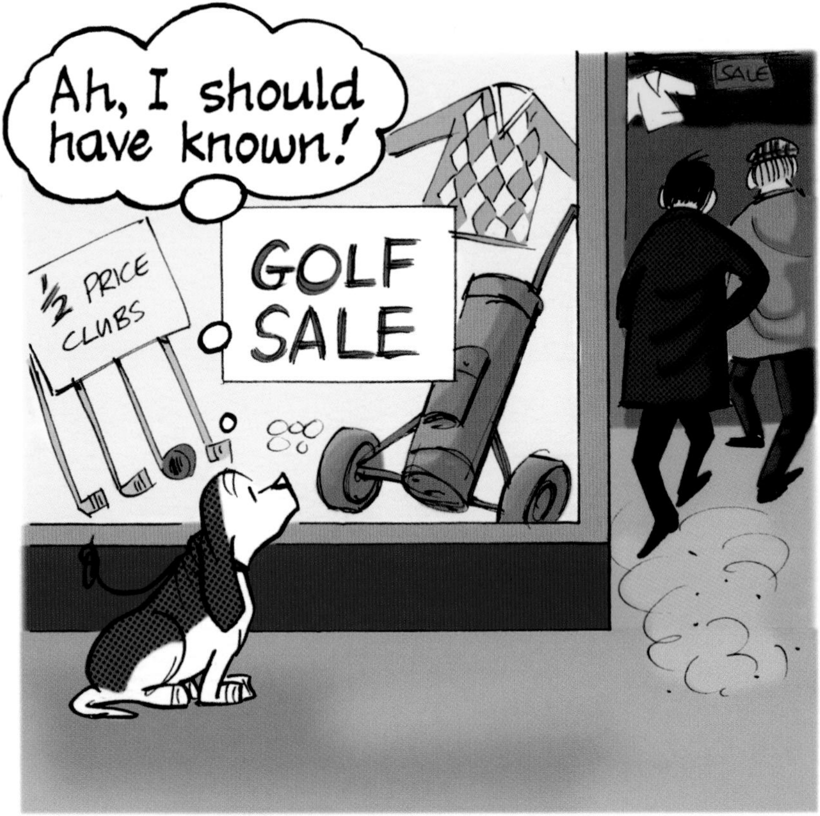
Ah, I should have known!
1/2 PRICE CLUBS
GOLF SALE
SALE

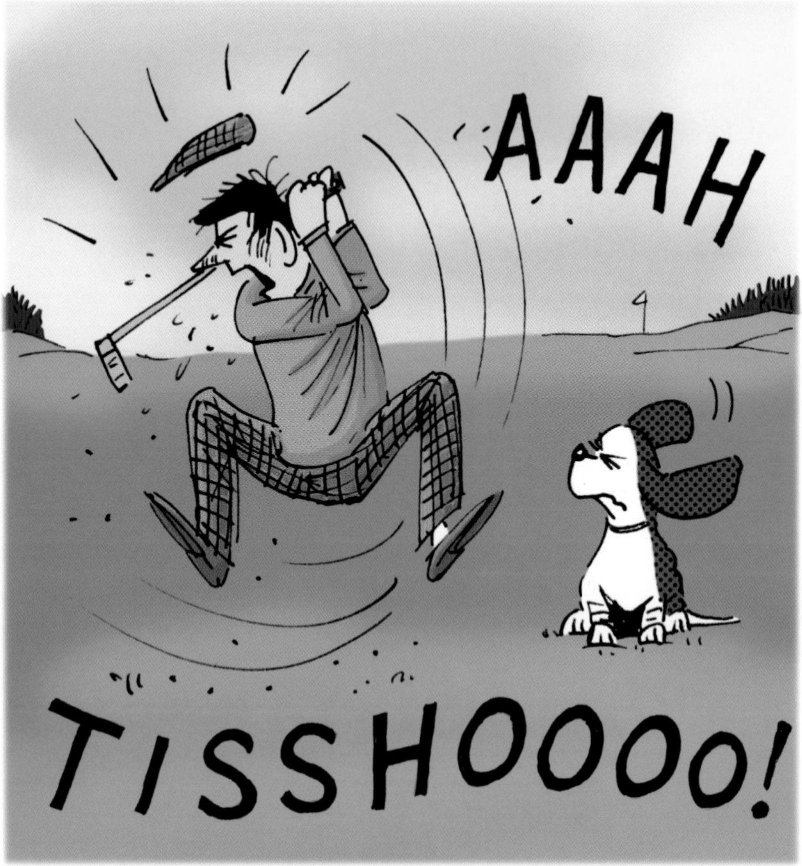
AAAH
TISSHOOOO!

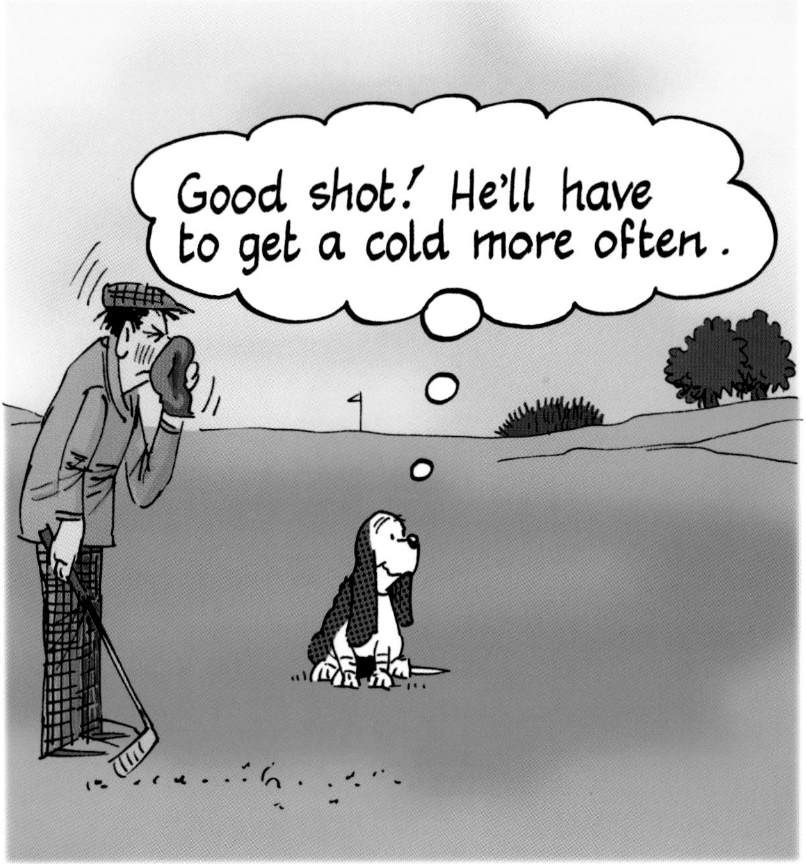
Good shot! He'll have to get a cold more often.

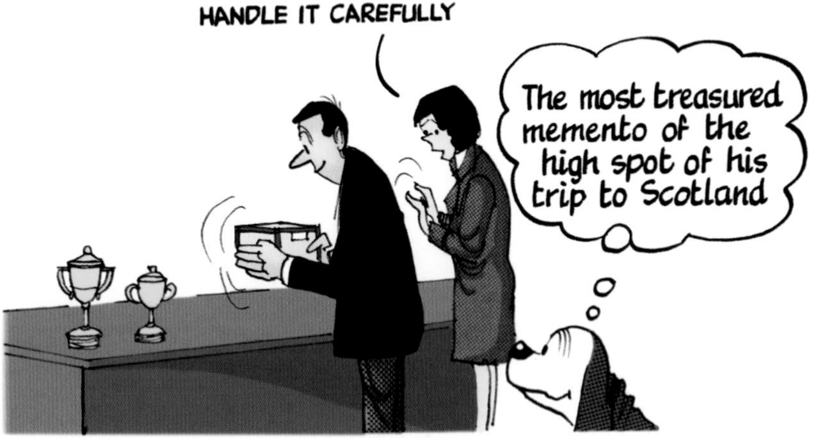
HANDLE IT CAREFULLY
The most treasured memento of the high spot of his trip to Scotland

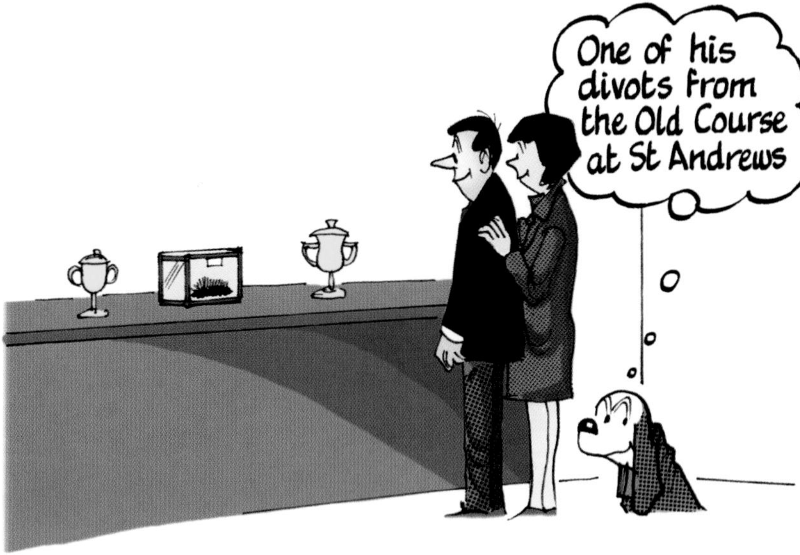
One of his divots from the Old Course at St Andrews

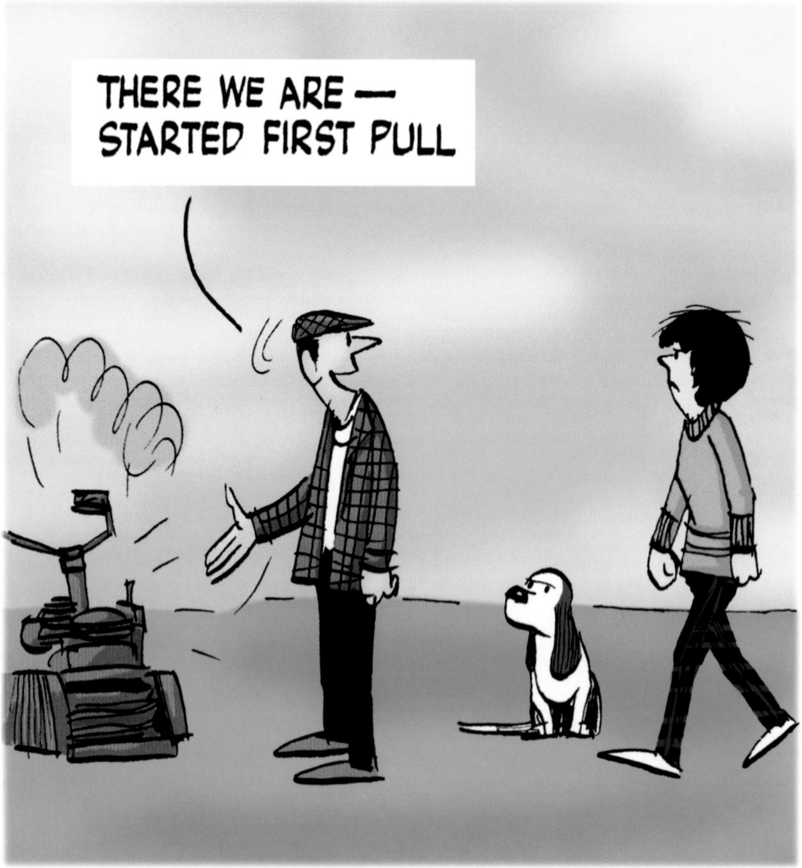
THERE WE ARE —
STARTED FIRST PULL

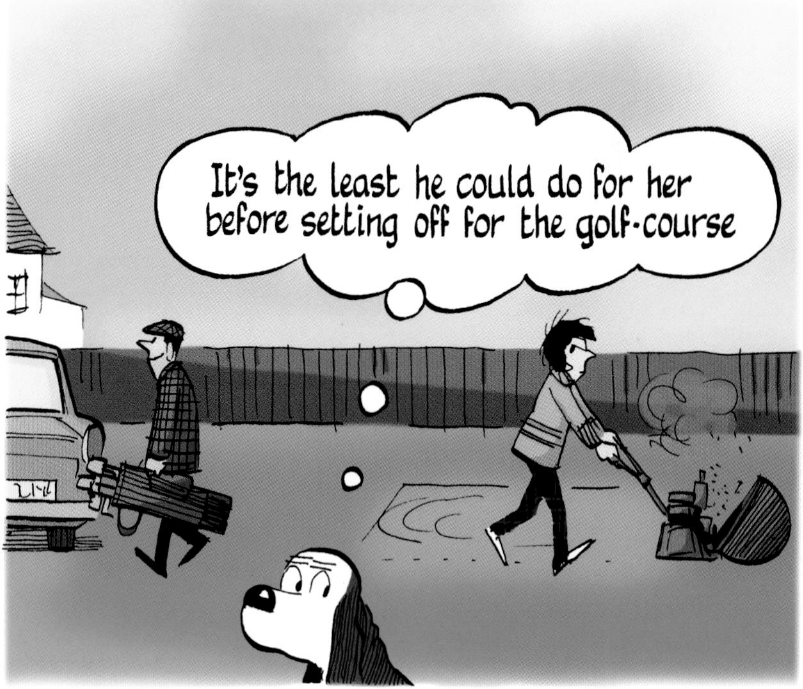
It's the least he could do for her before setting off for the golf-course

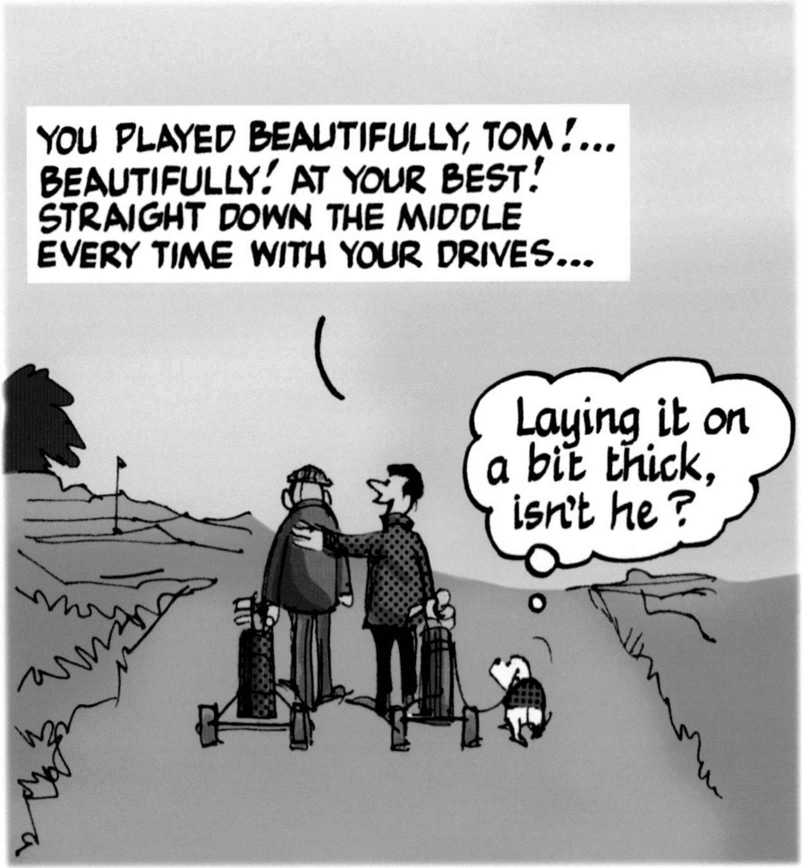
YOU PLAYED BEAUTIFULLY, TOM!... BEAUTIFULLY! AT YOUR BEST! STRAIGHT DOWN THE MIDDLE EVERY TIME WITH YOUR DRIVES...
Laying it on a bit thick, isn't he?

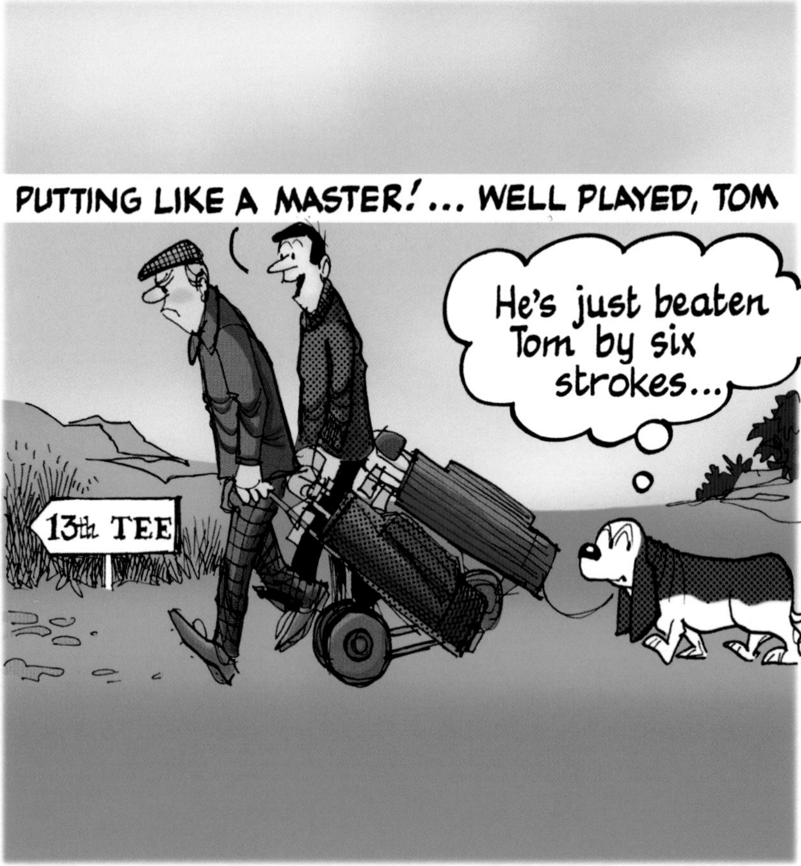
PUTTING LIKE A MASTER! ... WELL PLAYED, TOM
He's just beaten Tom by six strokes...
13th TEE

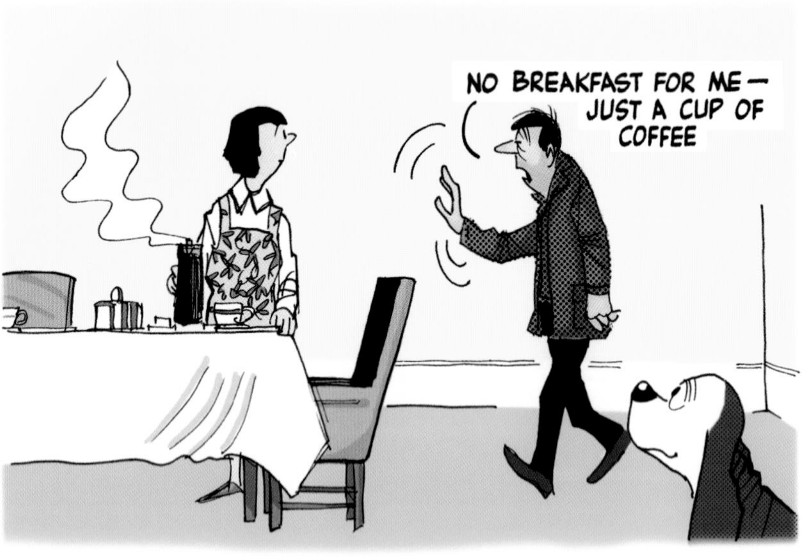
NO BREAKFAST FOR ME — JUST A CUP OF COFFEE

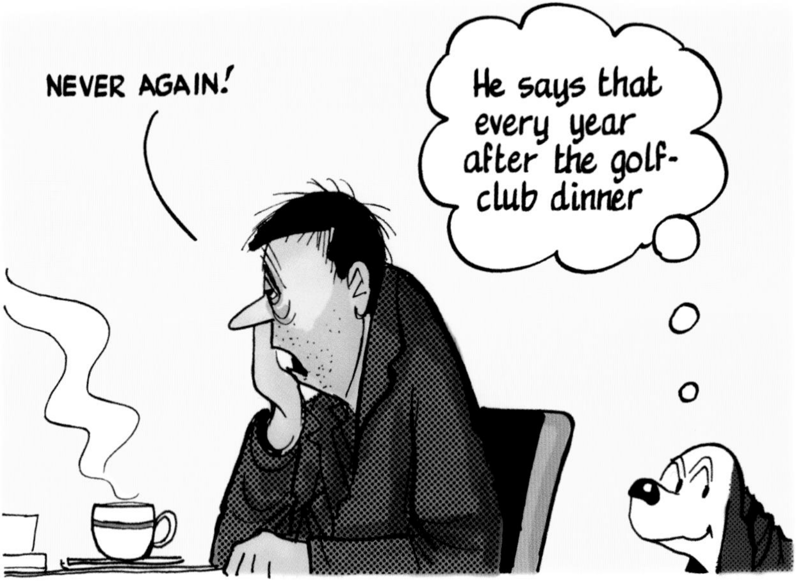
NEVER AGAIN!
He says that every year after the golf-club dinner

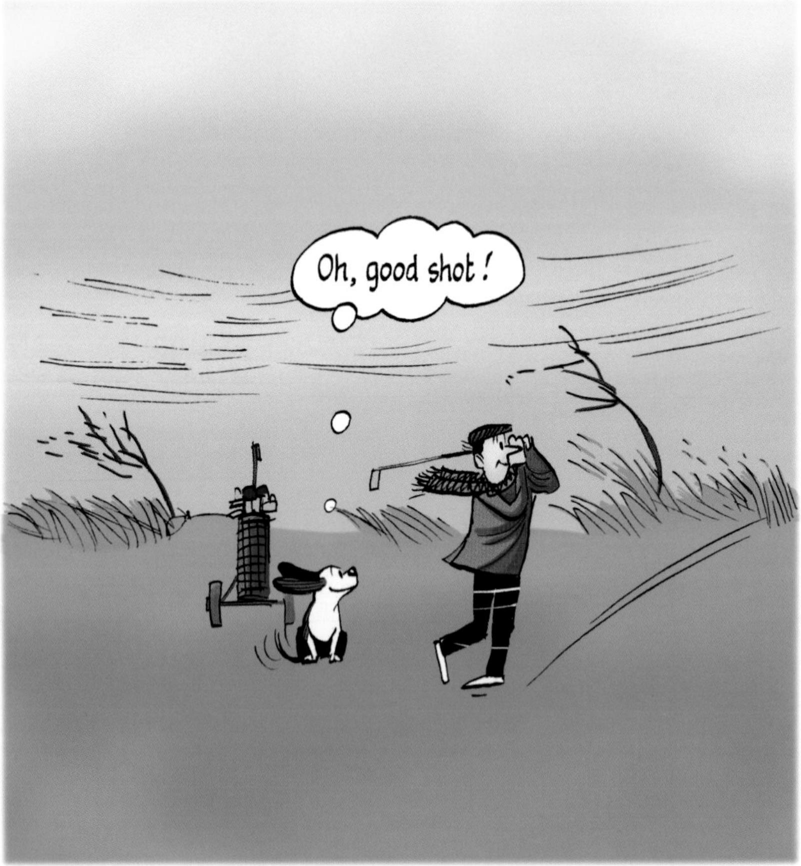
Oh, good shot!

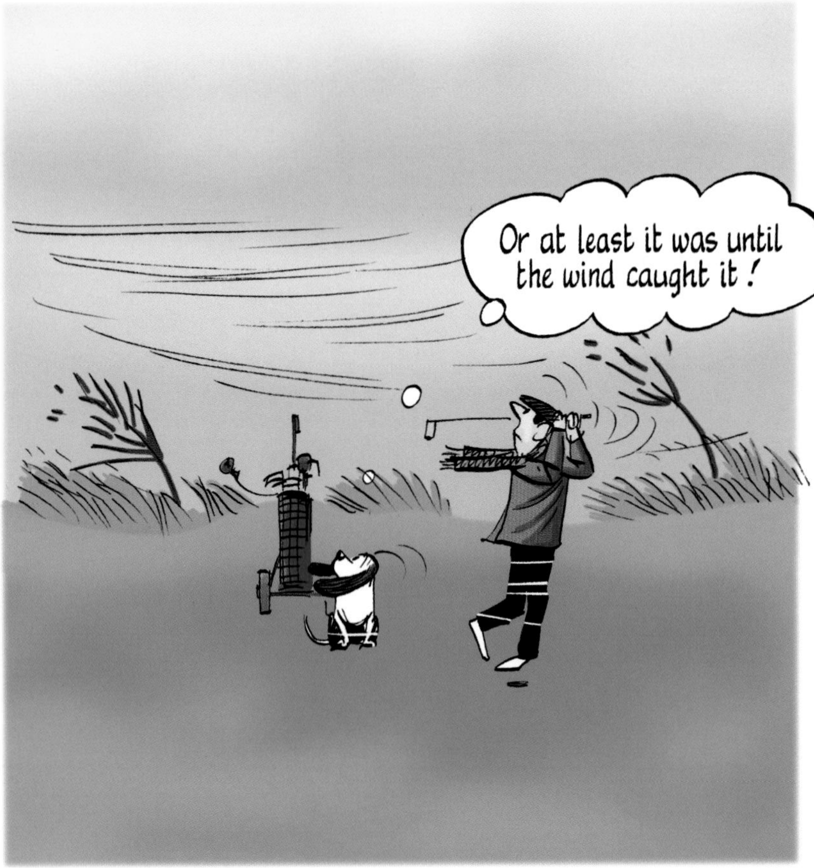
Or at least it was until the wind caught it!

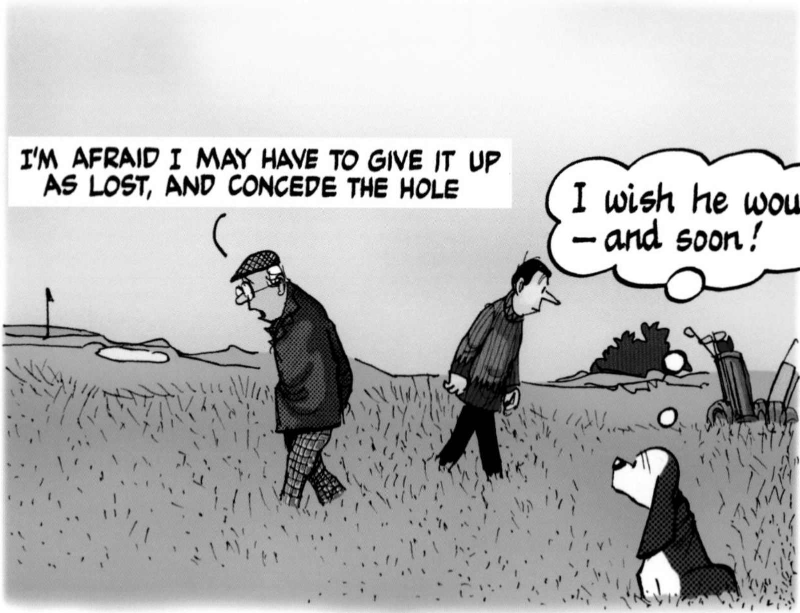
I'M AFRAID I MAY HAVE TO GIVE IT UP AS LOST, AND CONCEDE THE HOLE
I wish he would – and soon!

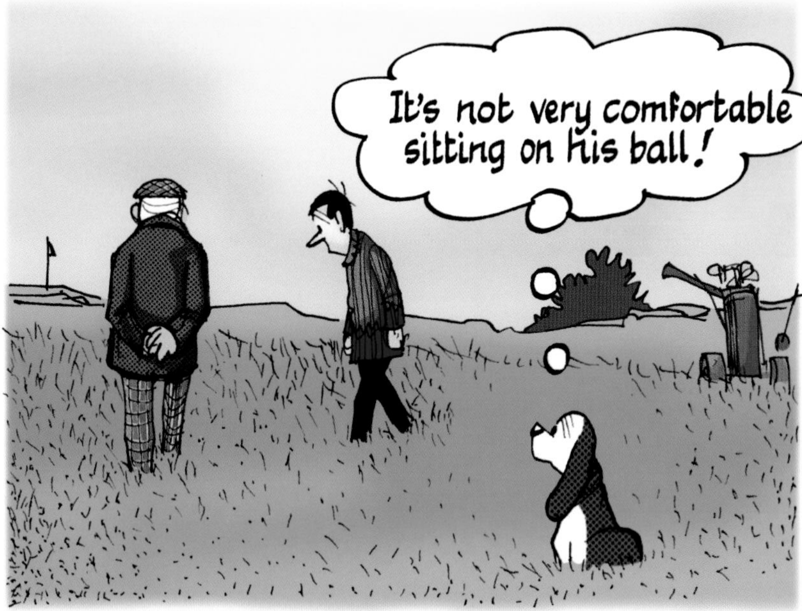
It's not very comfortable sitting on his ball!

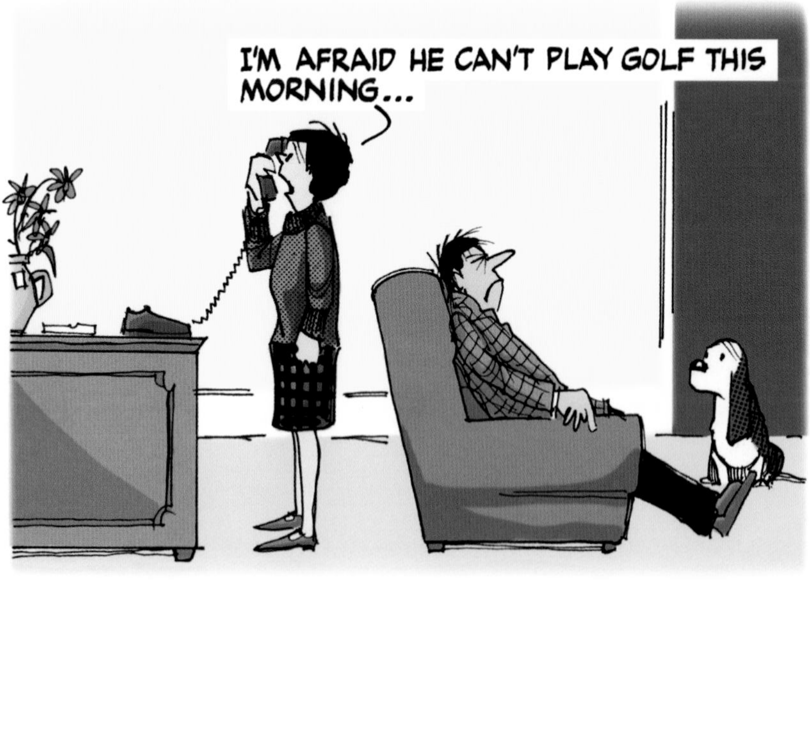
I'M AFRAID HE CAN'T PLAY GOLF THIS MORNING...

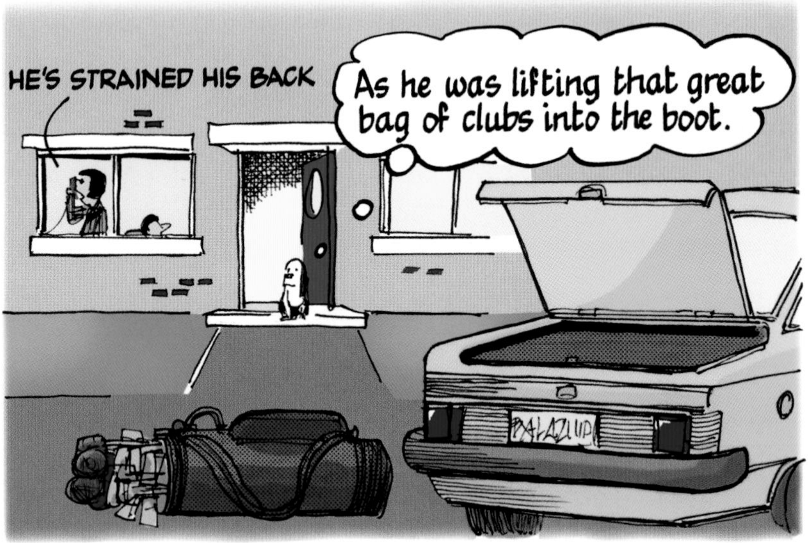
HE'S STRAINED HIS BACK
As he was lifting that great bag of clubs into the boot.

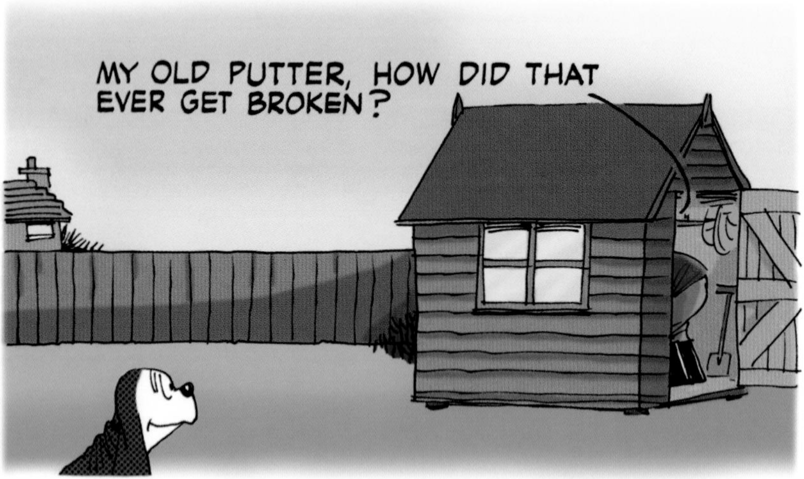
MY OLD PUTTER, HOW DID THAT EVER GET BROKEN?

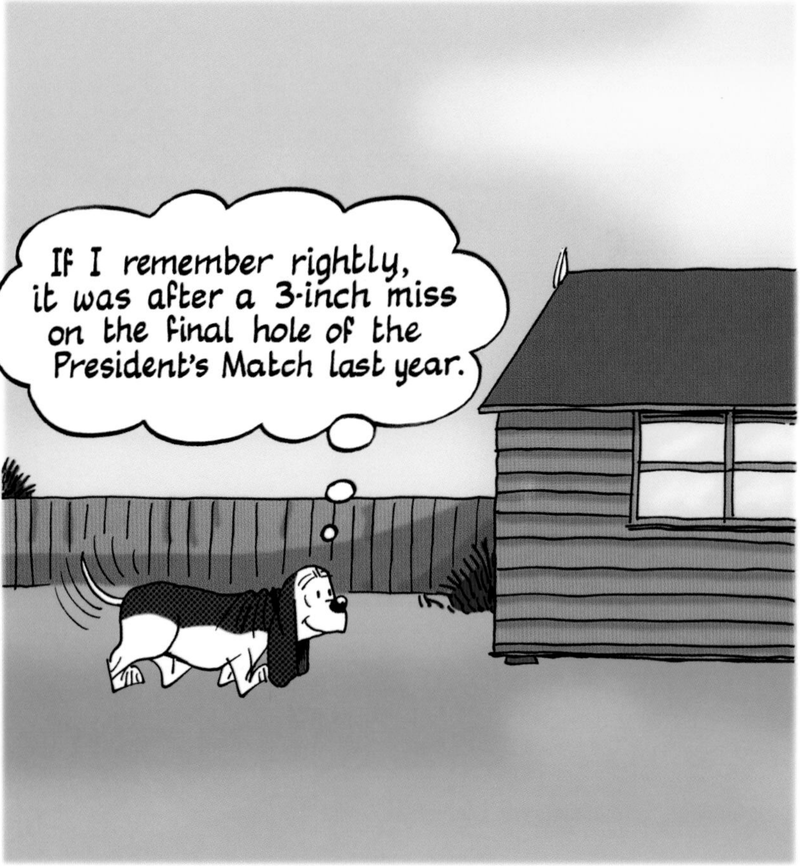
If I remember rightly, it was after a 3-inch miss on the final hole of the President's Match last year.

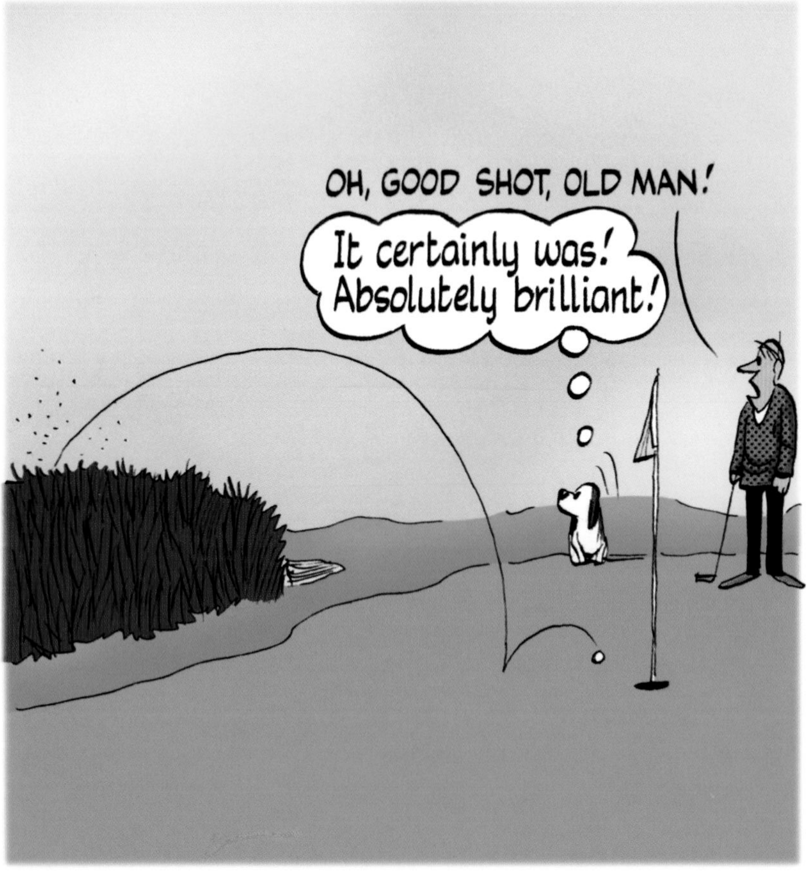

OH, GOOD SHOT, OLD MAN!
It certainly was! Absolutely brilliant!

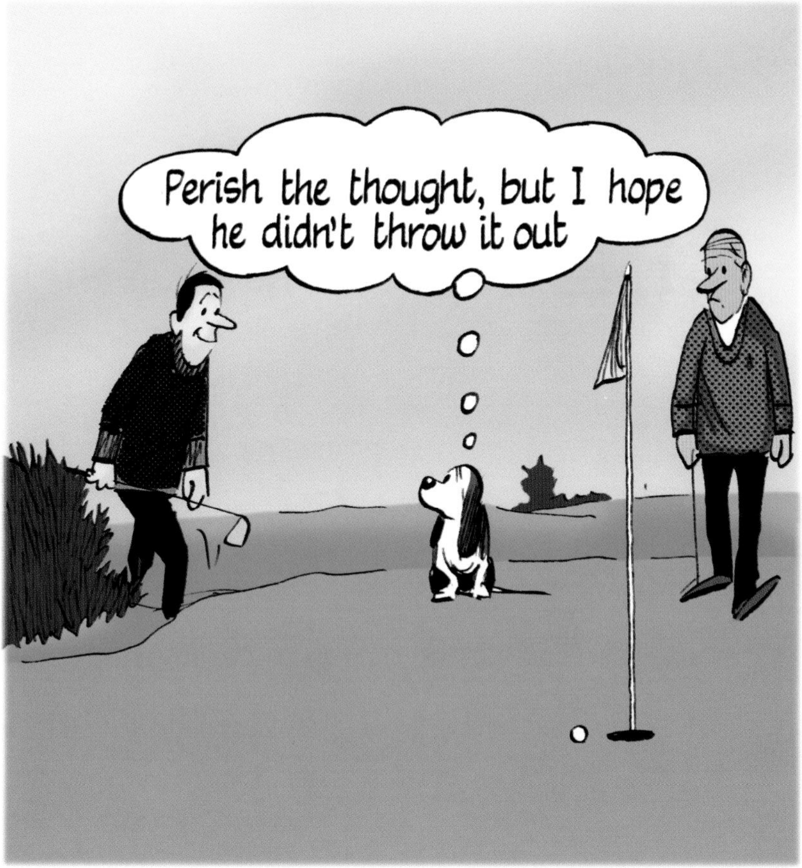
Perish the thought, but I hope he didn't throw it out

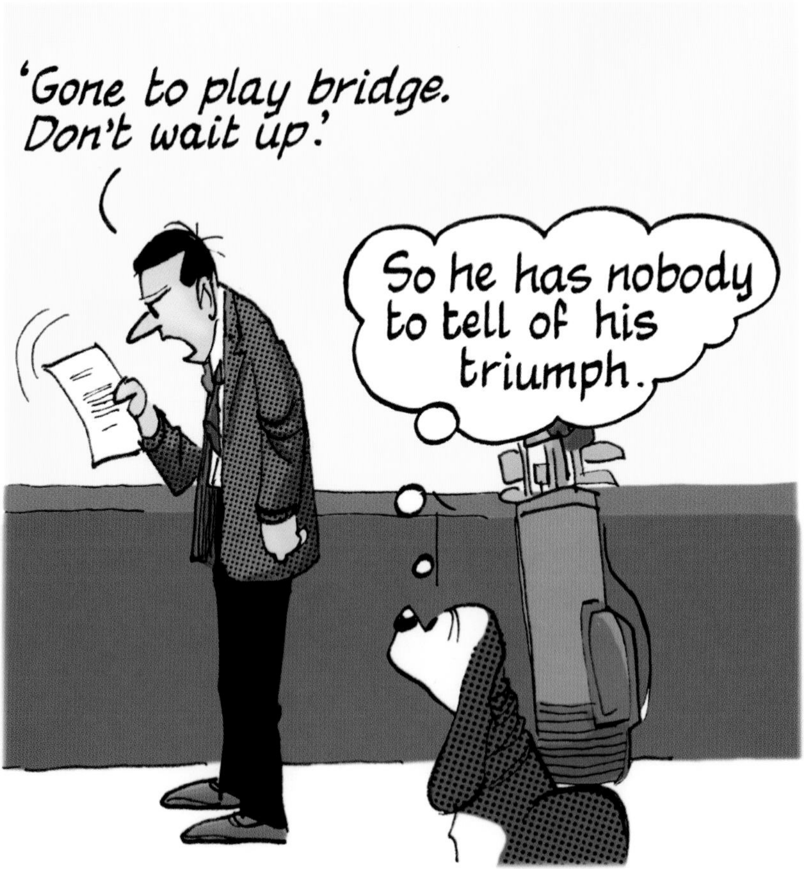
'Gone to play bridge.
Don't wait up.'
So he has nobody
to tell of his
triumph.

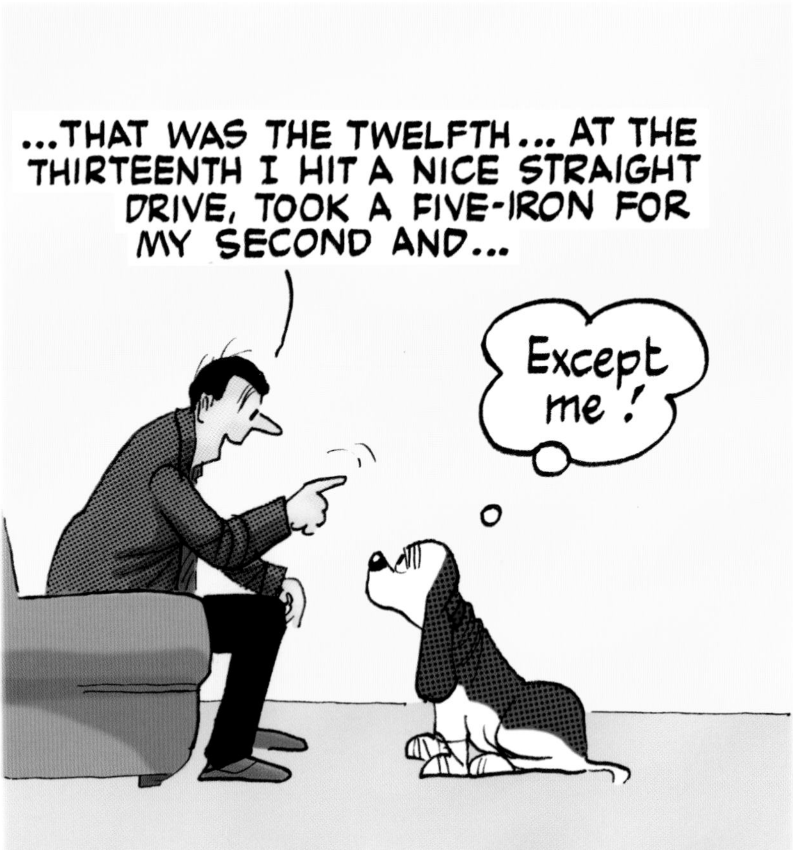
...THAT WAS THE TWELFTH... AT THE THIRTEENTH I HIT A NICE STRAIGHT DRIVE, TOOK A FIVE-IRON FOR MY SECOND AND...
Except me!

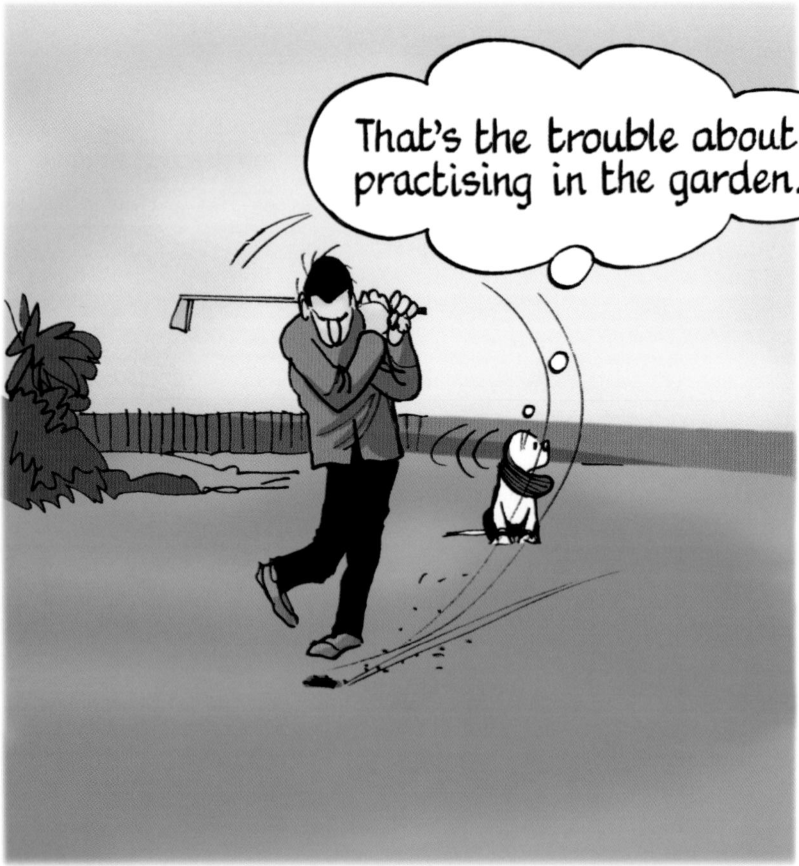
That's the trouble about practising in the garden...

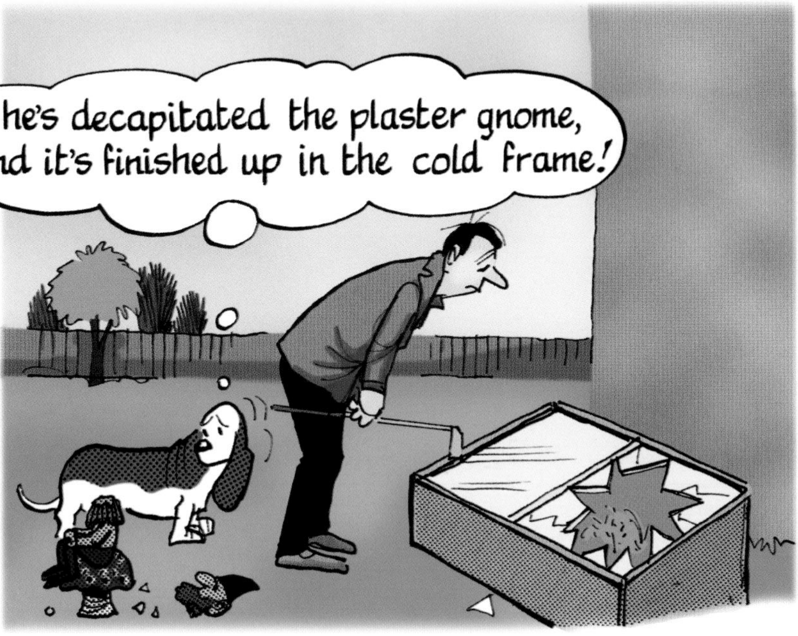
... he's decapitated the plaster gnome, and it's finished up in the cold frame!

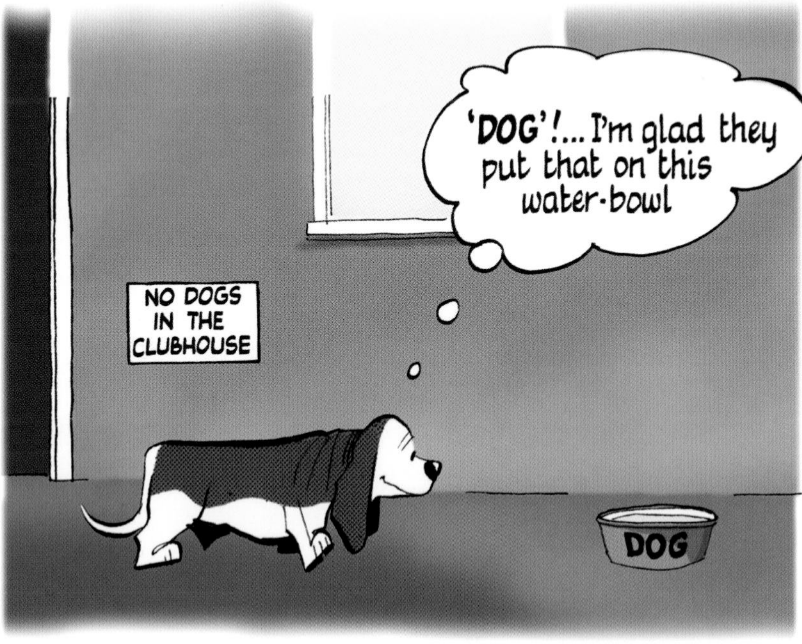
'DOG'!... I'm glad they put that on this water-bowl
NO DOGS IN THE CLUBHOUSE
DOG

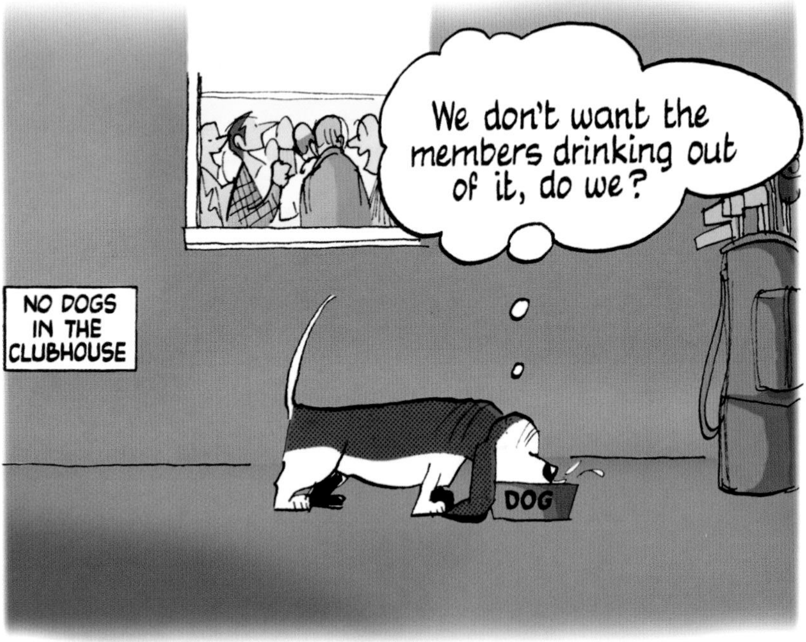
We don't want the members drinking out of it, do we?
NO DOGS IN THE CLUBHOUSE
DOG

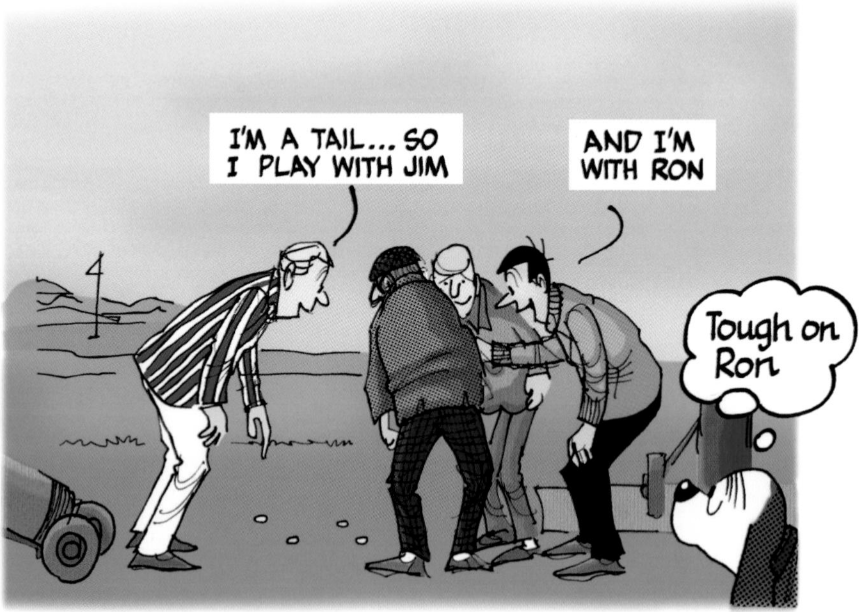
I'M A TAIL... SO
I PLAY WITH JIM
AND I'M
WITH RON
Tough on
Ron

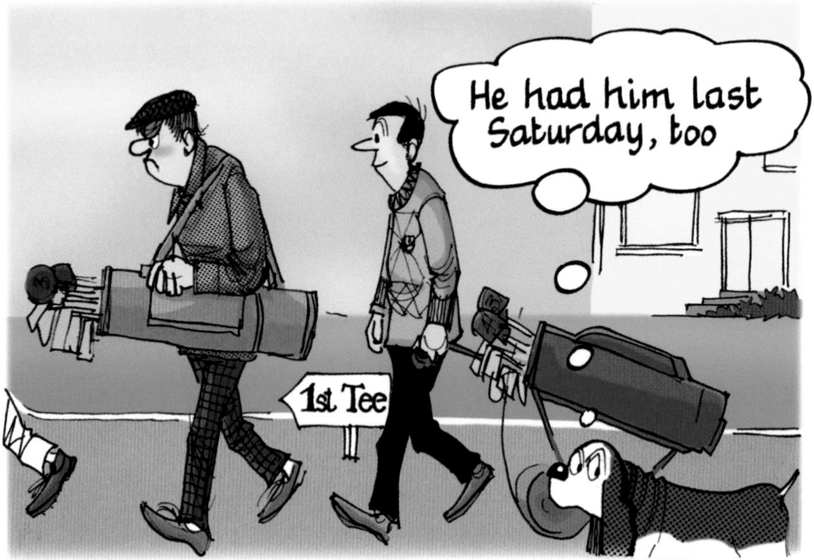
1st Tee
He had him last Saturday, too

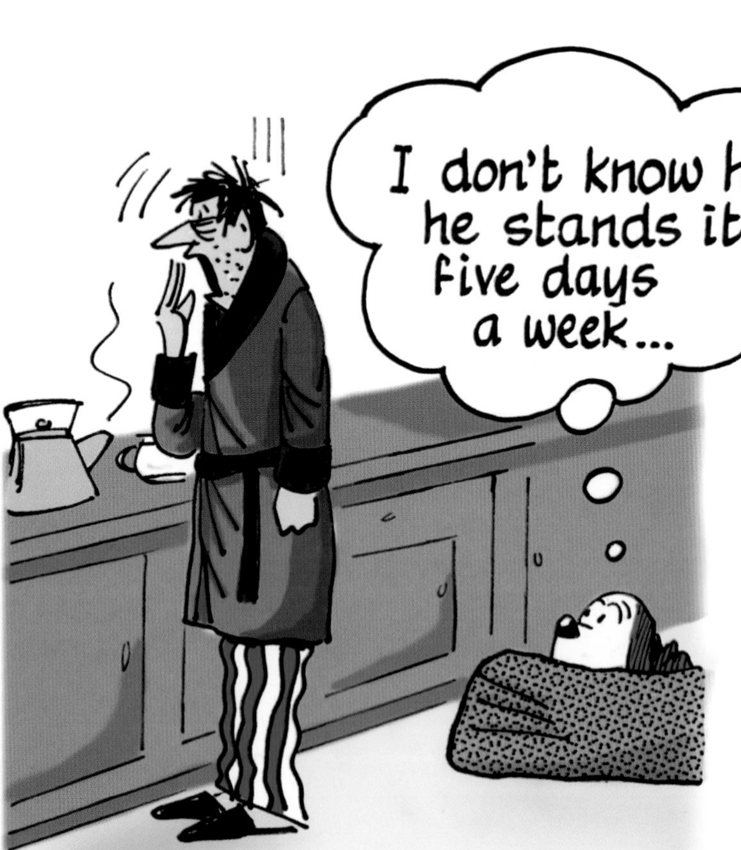
I don't know how he stands it, five days a week...

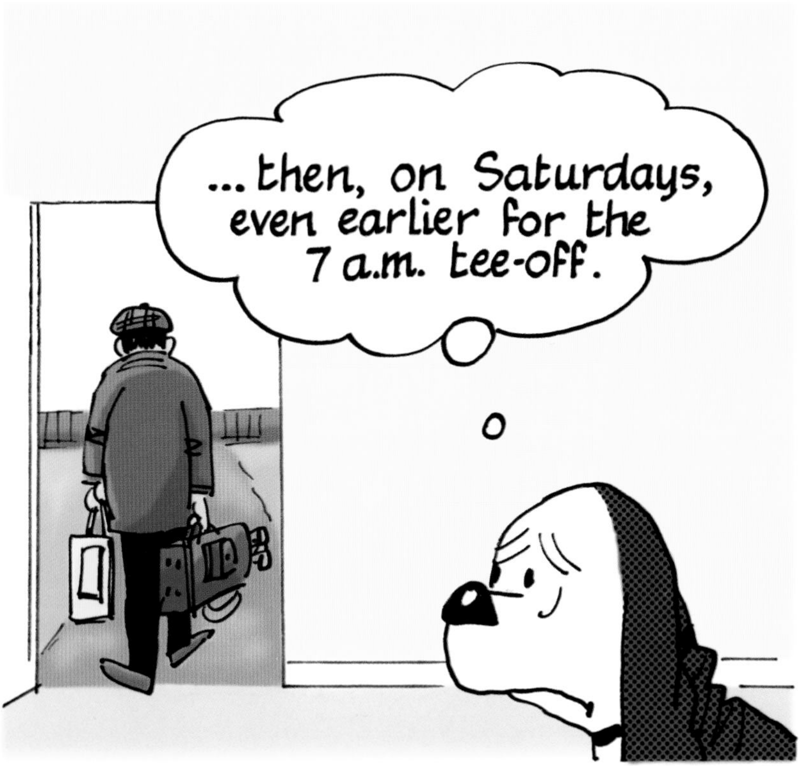
...then, on Saturdays, even earlier for the 7 a.m. tee-off.

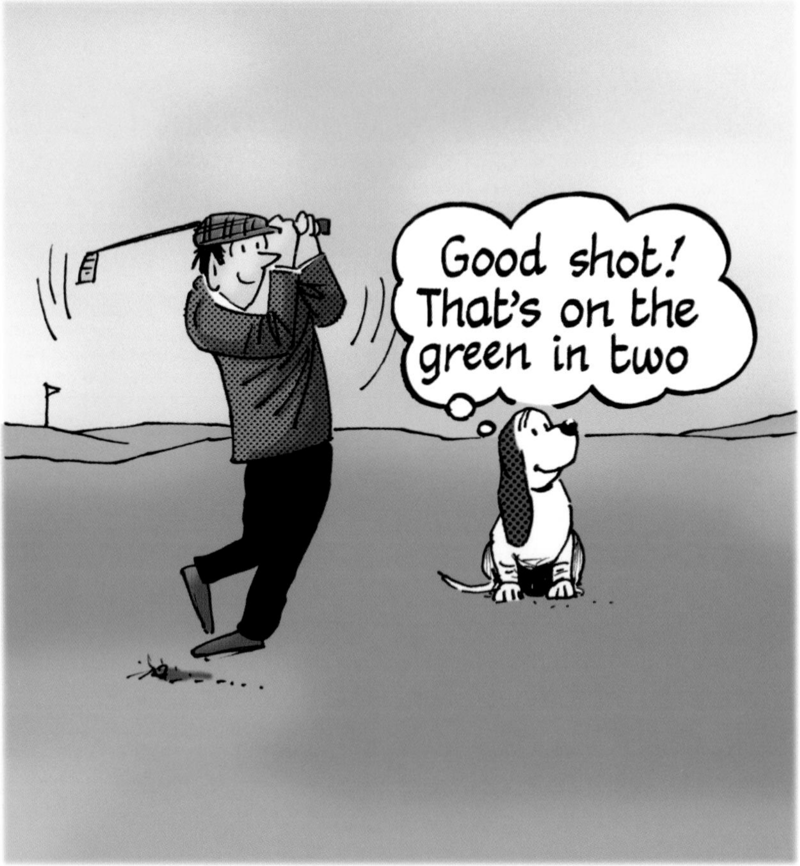
Good shot! That's on the green in two

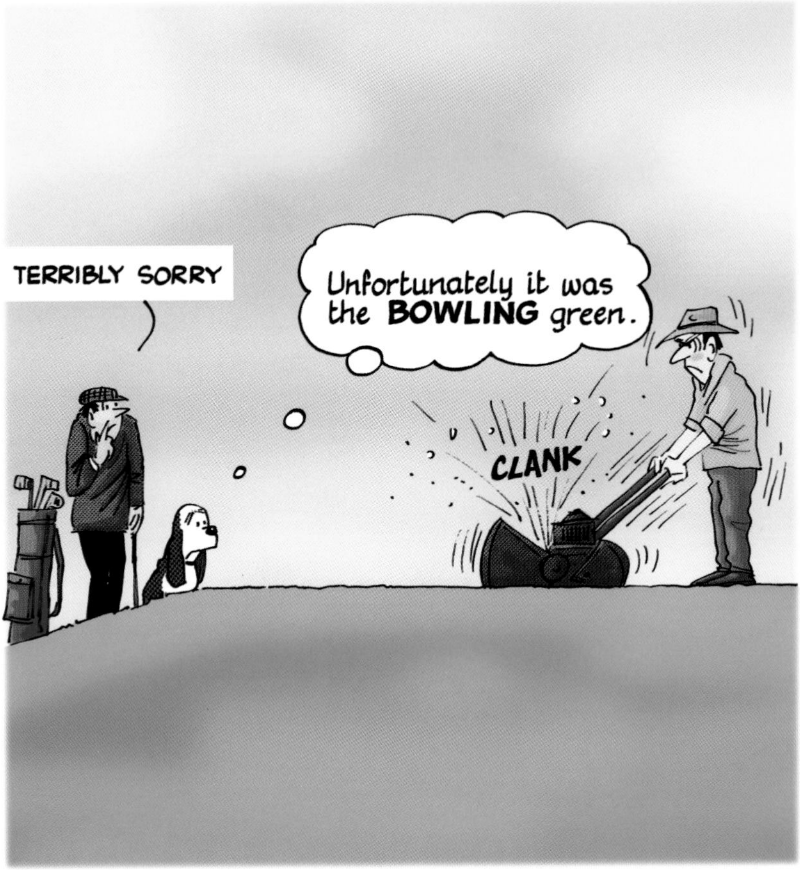

TERRIBLY SORRY
Unfortunately it was the BOWLING green.
CLANK

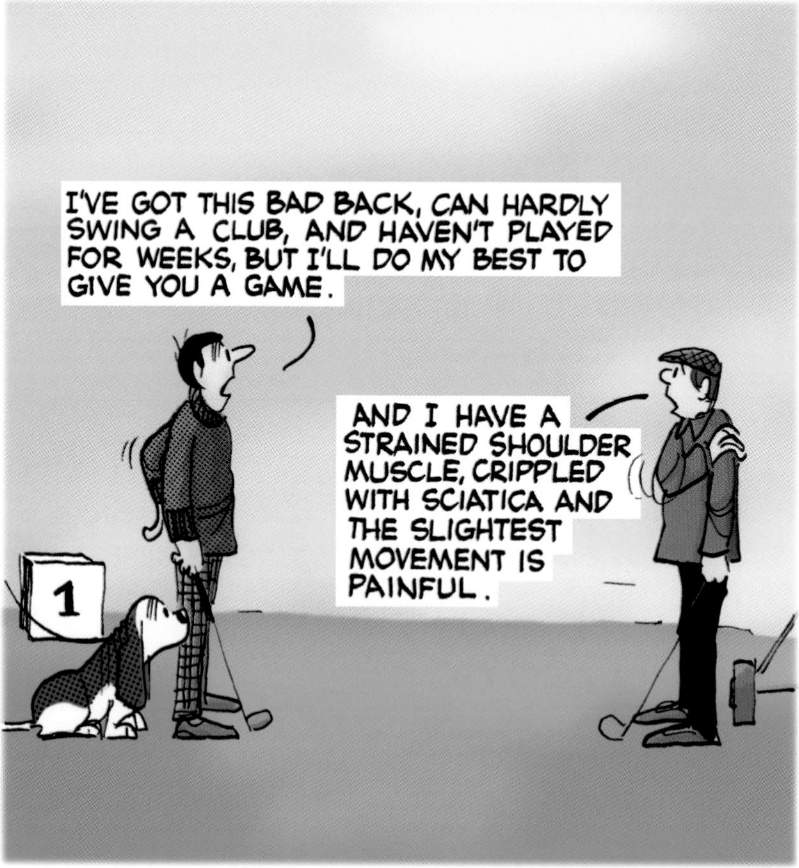
I'VE GOT THIS BAD BACK, CAN HARDLY SWING A CLUB, AND HAVEN'T PLAYED FOR WEEKS, BUT I'LL DO MY BEST TO GIVE YOU A GAME.
AND I HAVE A STRAINED SHOULDER MUSCLE, CRIPPLED WITH SCIATICA AND THE SLIGHTEST MOVEMENT IS PAINFUL.
1

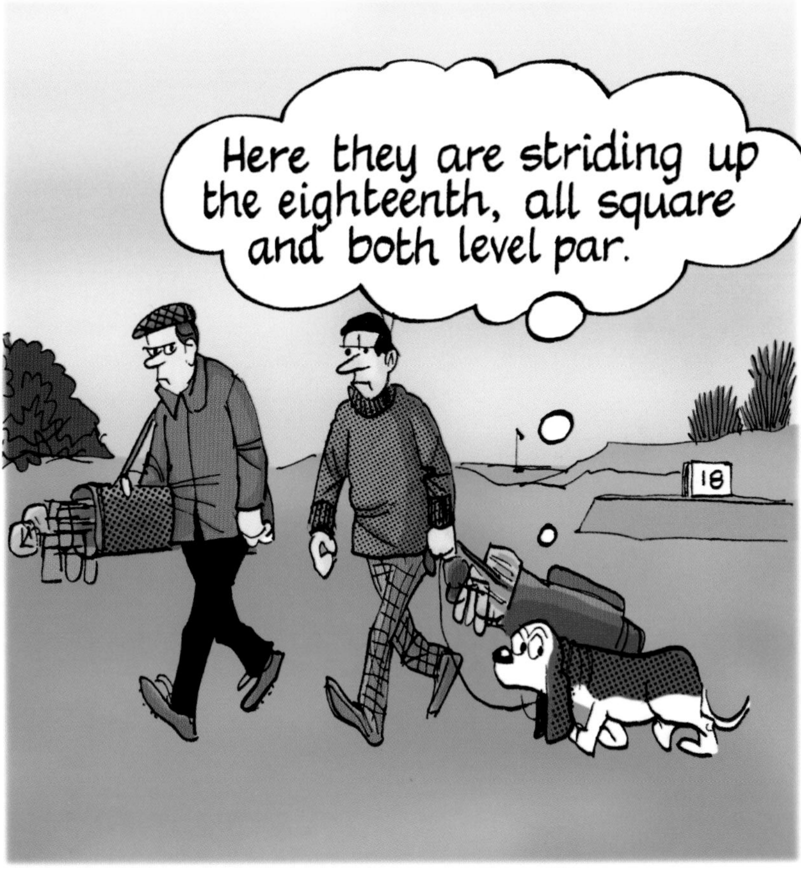
Here they are striding up the eighteenth, all square and both level par.
18

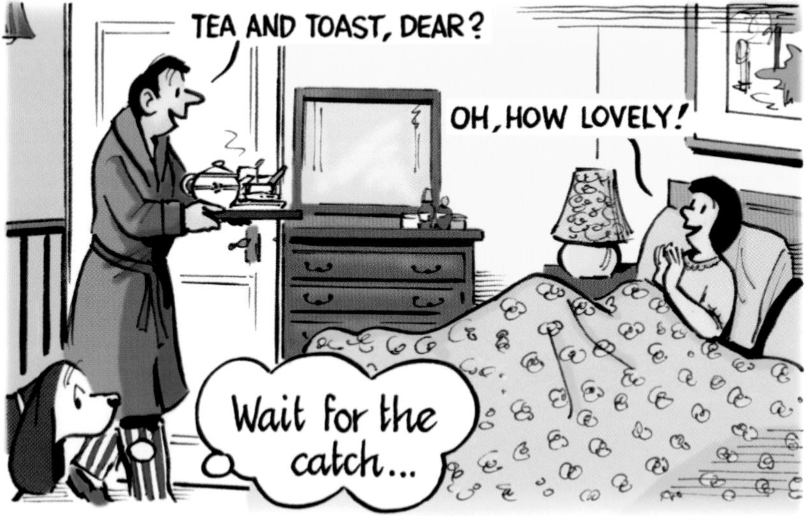
TEA AND TOAST, DEAR?
OH, HOW LOVELY!
Wait for the catch...

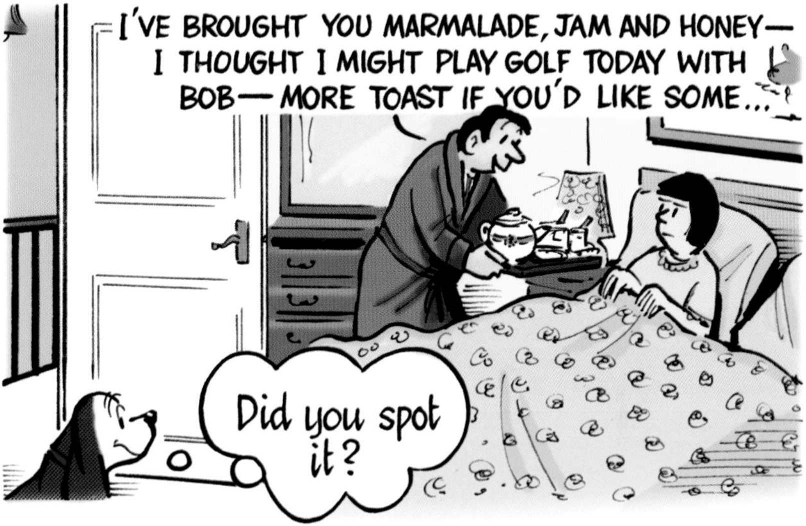
I'VE BROUGHT YOU MARMALADE, JAM AND HONEY— I THOUGHT I MIGHT PLAY GOLF TODAY WITH BOB— MORE TOAST IF YOU'D LIKE SOME...
Did you spot it?

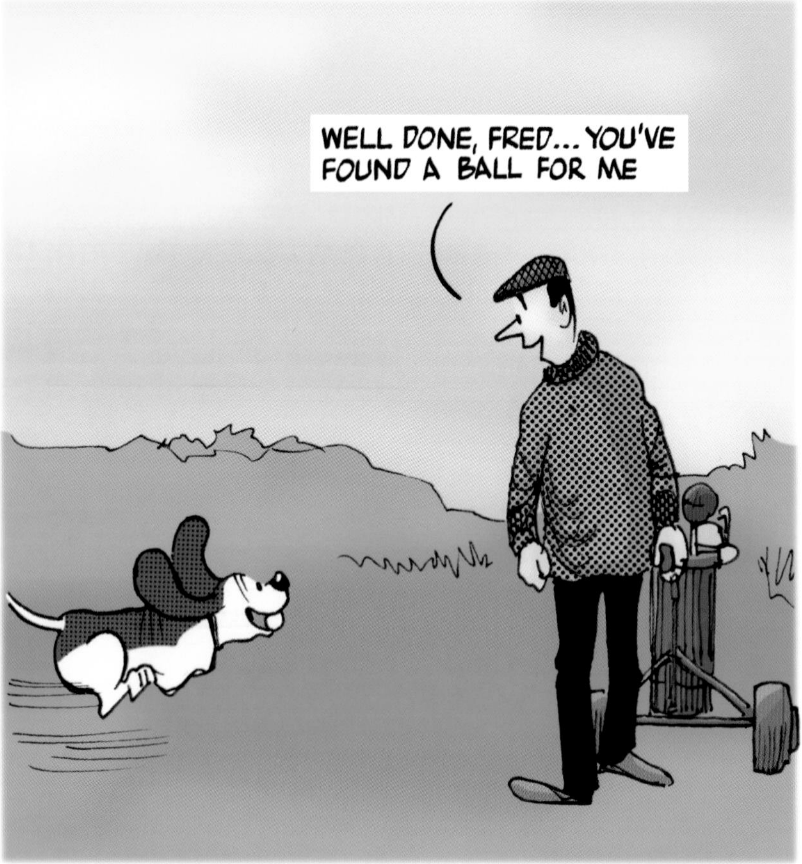
WELL DONE, FRED... YOU'VE FOUND A BALL FOR ME

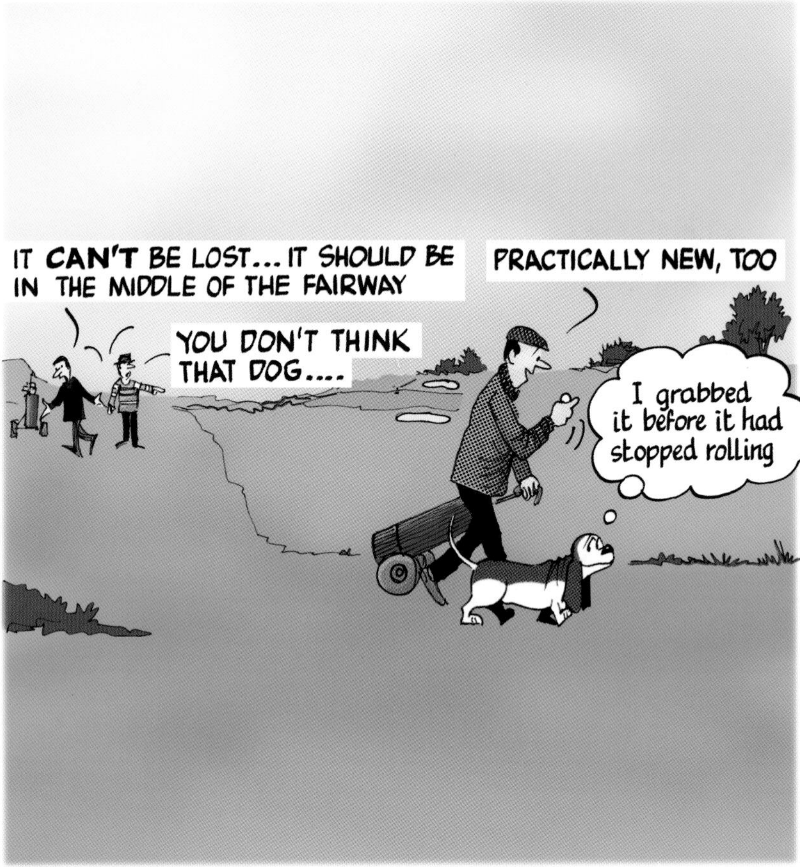
IT CAN'T BE LOST... IT SHOULD BE IN THE MIDDLE OF THE FAIRWAY
YOU DON'T THINK THAT DOG....
PRACTICALLY NEW, TOO
I grabbed it before it had stopped rolling

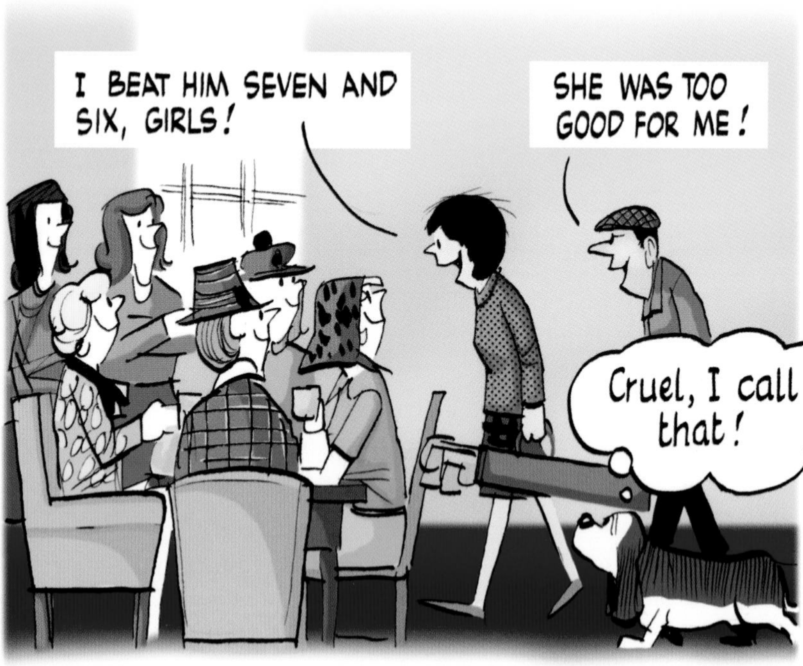
I BEAT HIM SEVEN AND SIX, GIRLS!
SHE WAS TOO GOOD FOR ME!
Cruel, I call that!

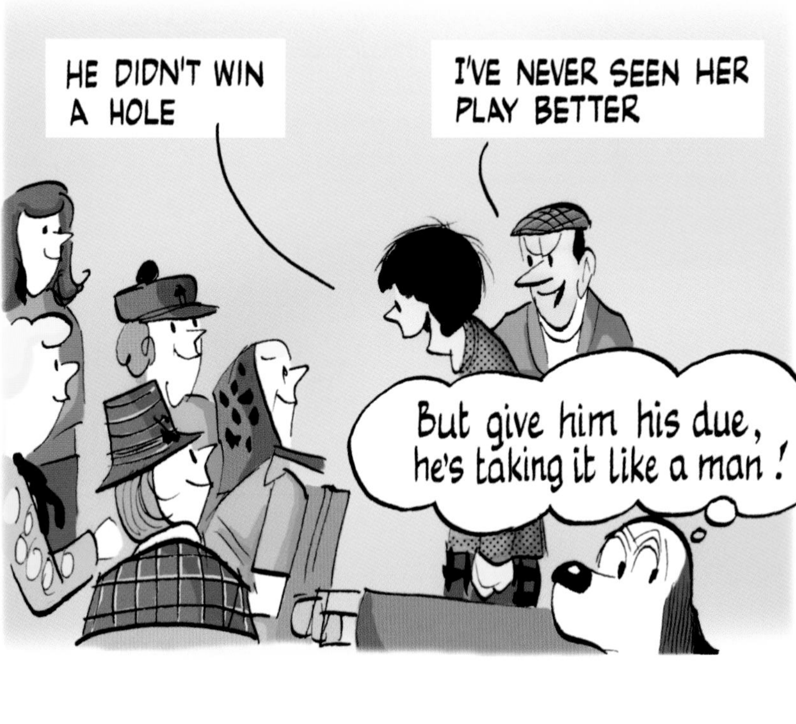
HE DIDN'T WIN A HOLE
I'VE NEVER SEEN HER PLAY BETTER
But give him his due, he's taking it like a man!

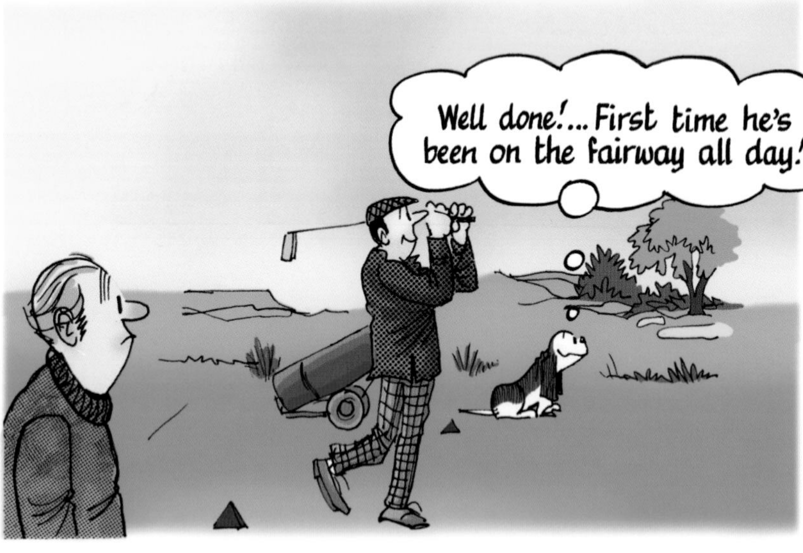
Well done!... First time he's been on the fairway all day!

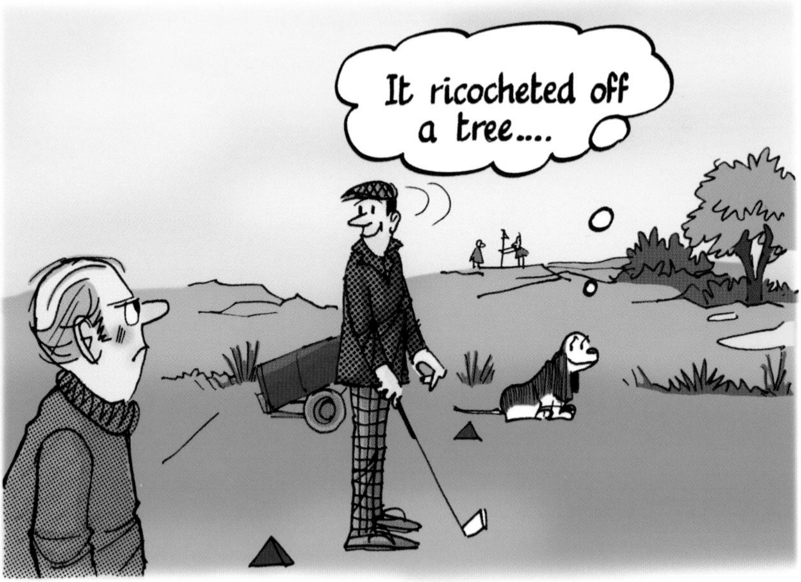

It ricocheted off a tree....

WE'RE OFF TO THE GOLF CLUB DINNER-DANCE AND YOU'RE THE GUEST OF HONOUR.

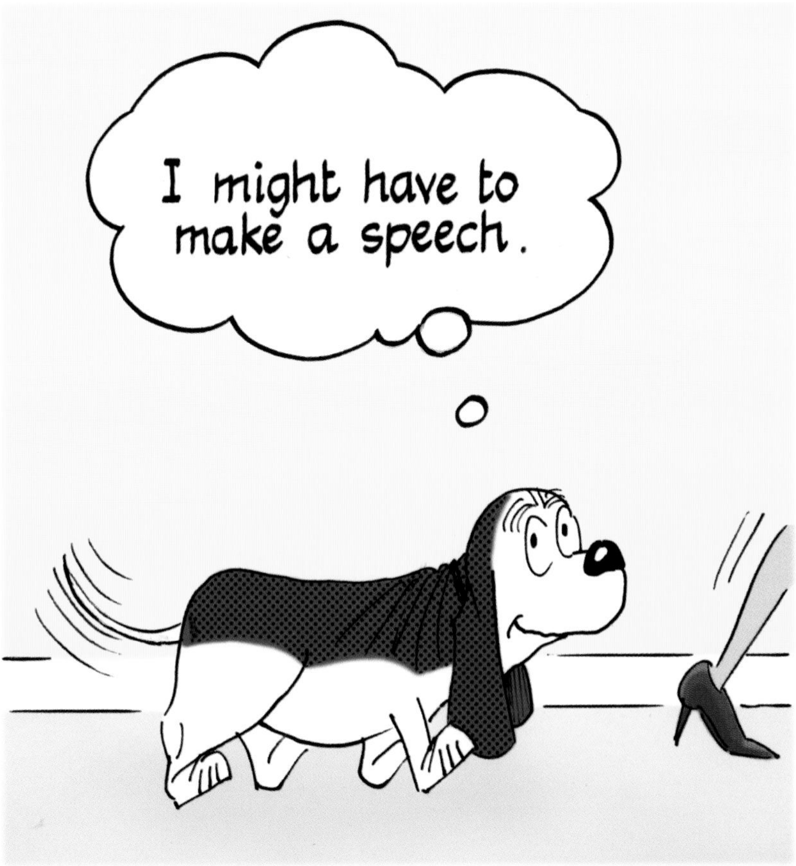
I might have to make a speech.

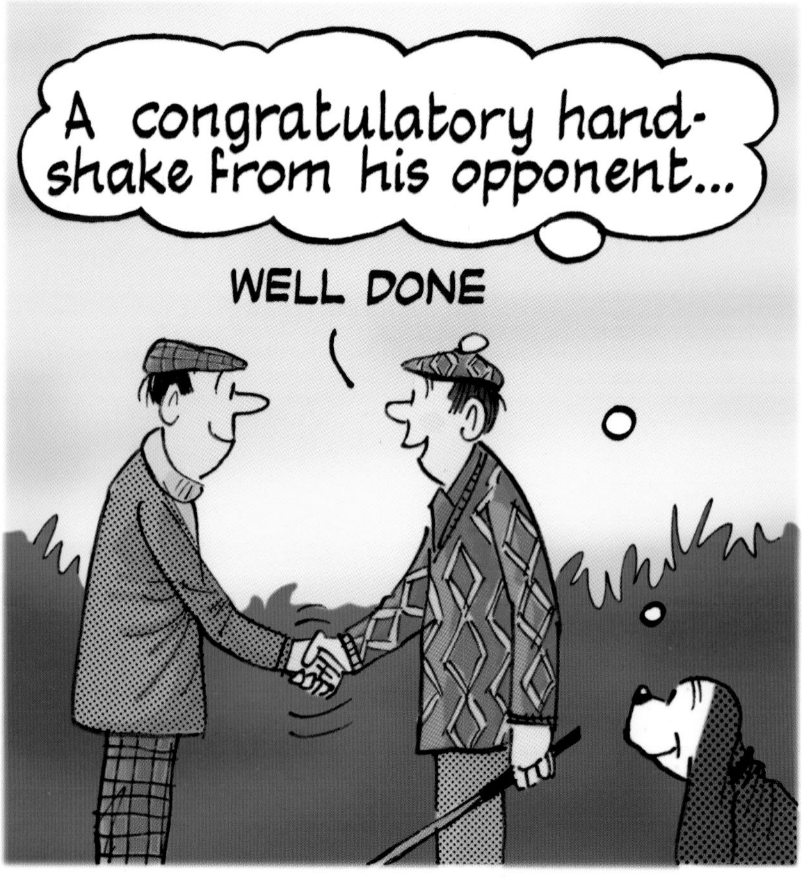
A congratulatory hand-shake from his opponent...
WELL DONE

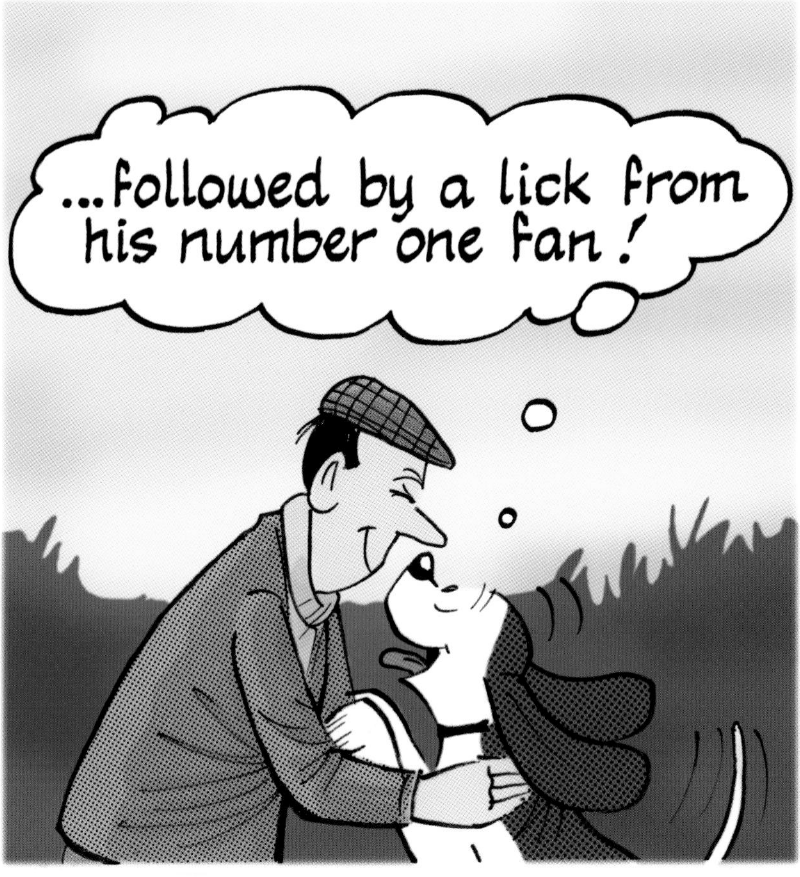
...followed by a lick from his number one fan!

Look out for other gift books featuring the one and only Fred Basset...

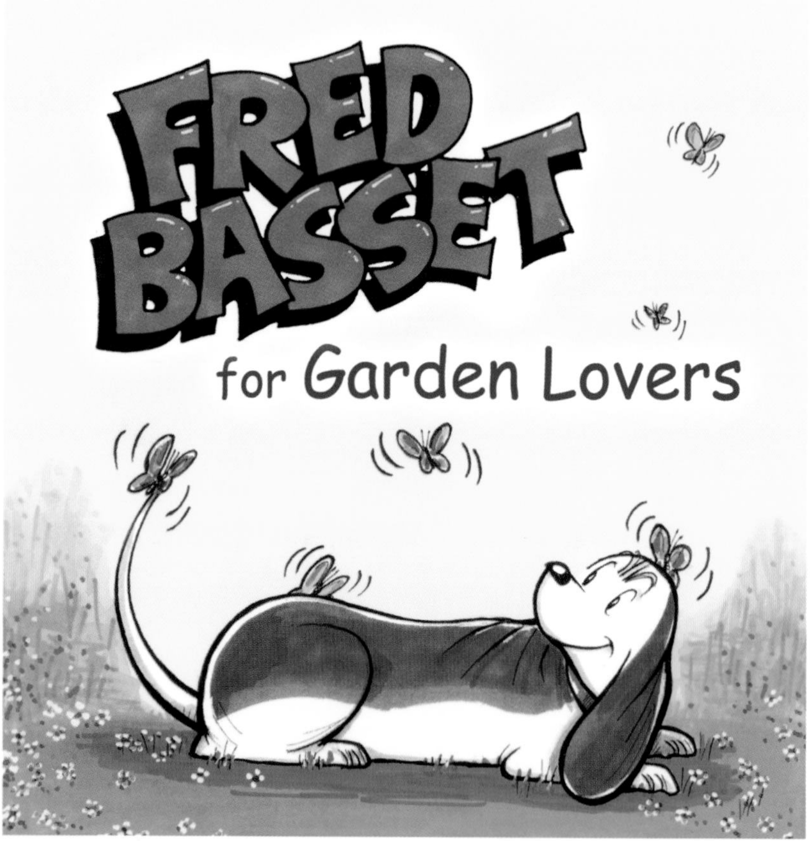
FRED BASSET
for Garden Lovers

Fred Basset for Garden Lovers

ISBN: 978 1 84024 779 4

Hardback

£5.99

There is lots of fun to be had by a dog in a garden – especially if your name is Fred Basset!

Whether he's lazing on the lawn, chasing next door's cat or hunting down a long-lost bone, Fred's antics and astute observations on humans will keep you entertained for hours.

Have you enjoyed this book? If so, why not
write a review on your favourite website?

Thanks very much for buying
this Summersdale book.

www.summersdale.com

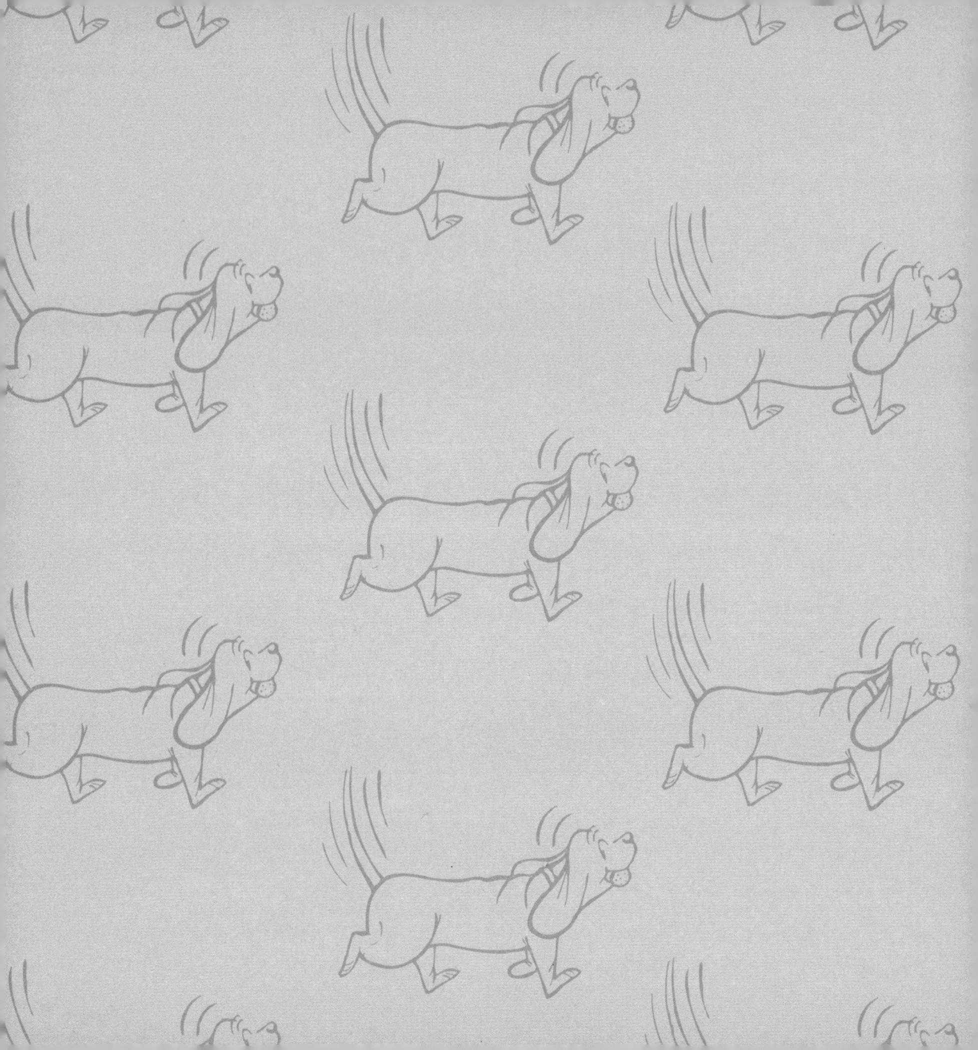

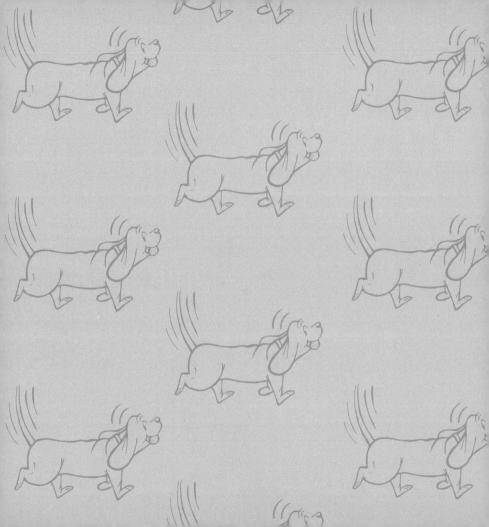